"About ten days after 9/11, I went through the Pentagon and I saw Secretary Rumsfeld and Deputy Secretary Wolfowitz. I went downstairs just to say hello to some of the people on the Joint Staff who used to work for me, and one of the generals called me in. He said, 'Sir, you've got to come in and talk to me a second.' I said, 'Well, you're too busy.' He said, 'No, no.' He says, 'We've made the decision we're going to war with Iraq.' This was on or about the twentieth of September...

"So I came back to see him a few weeks later, and by that time we were bombing in Afghanistan. I said, 'Are we still going to war with Iraq?' And he said, 'Oh, it's worse than that.' He reached over on his desk. He picked up a piece of paper. And he said, 'I just got this down from upstairs'—meaning the Secretary of Defense's office—'today.' And he said, 'This is a memo that describes how we're going to take out seven countries in five years.'"

—*General Wesley Clark, February 27, 2007*

IRAN

Iran is working to develop tactical nuclear capabilities, abetting attacks against U.S. forces in Iraq and Afghanistan, and building relationships with known terrorist groups. Decisive and direct action must be taken.

ABSTRACT

- The Islamic Republic of Iran is an oppressive and theocratically absolutist regime, and has dedicated itself to promoting unrest and conflict in neighboring countries. Its ultimate goal is regional domination.

- Iran seeks to destabilize both Afghanistan and Iraq as part of an overall effort to assert influence on those nations.

- Iran is known to support, both financially and logistically, the most violent terrorist organizations in the region. It is actively working with Hamas and Hezbollah, as well as al Qaeda.

- Iran is currently working toward a fully operable nuclear weapon, in direct defiance of nonproliferation treaties.

- Possession of a nuclear weapon would encourage the Iranian government to defy the United States's diplomatic efforts. Worse, the weapon could be conveyed to one of the many terrorist organizations the country now funds, and used against Israel, Europe, or even the U.S.

- The intricate nature of Iran's governmental power structures renders it all but immune to conventional diplomacy. While the nation is ostensibly a republic, true leadership is monopolized by a shadowy cadre of ideologues, both elected and unelected.

INTRODUCTION

Without U.S. intervention, Iran will likely possess a nuclear weapon before the end of the decade. Given its antagonism toward the United States, the rhetoric of its present government, and its open support for anti-American terrorist organizations, this presents a catastrophic threat to our interests and to our citizens at home and abroad.

Iran's long-stated ambition is regional dominance. Possession of a nuclear weapon would almost certainly prompt it to act more decisively to attain this position, and increase its already dangerous levels of direct support for radical Islamic groups across the Middle East.

Our sanctions against Iran are maximized. Diplomacy has proven completely ineffective in dealing with the Iranian nuclear threat. There are no signs that Iran intends to voluntarily sever its connections to anti-American insurgents in Iraq and Afghanistan, or to non-state terrorist organizations like al Qaeda and Hezbollah. Every passing month indicates otherwise.

THREAT OVERVIEW

1. Revolution as Policy

Just as the Soviet Union pursued global communism, it is official Iranian foreign policy to actively and aggressively export its revolution. The

An Iranian tank factory

Iranian regime (see pg. 6) is considered by its leaders to be the only legitimate form of government anywhere in the world. Global Islamic theocracy based on the Shia interpretation of the Koran is their ideological core. Iranian foreign agents continue to agitate for revolutions in countries across the Middle East, through the use of special military forces and a web of tightly linked proxy organizations. The Iranian government is, and aims to be, a destabilizing force on the world stage.

2. An Ally to Terror

Today, Iran is the world's main state supporter of terrorism. Hezbollah has been armed and trained by Iran, and Iran continues to offer it arms shipments and spiritual guidance. Hamas receives a large portion of its funding from Iran, despite being a Sunni terrorist organization, as does the anti-Turkish Kurdistan Workers' Party (PKK) and the anti-American Iraqi agitator Moktada al-Sadr, whose militia is almost entirely

The Islamic Revolutionary Guard Corps

funded and armed by Iranian agents. Moktada's militia is responsible for many of the American military deaths in Iraq, and for the Shia death squads fueling much of the sectarian violence undermining the creation of a peaceful, unified Iraqi state.

Iran also has a history of support for al Qaeda. While the two groups have different goals for the region, they have joined together on matters of mutual security. Iran is presently giving sanctuary to high-ranking al Qaeda members as part of a larger agreement.

One of the main conduits of Iran's support of these entities is its Islamic Revolutionary Guard Corps (IRGC). The IRGC is a special ideological fighting force, roughly one hundred and twenty-five thousand strong, entrusted with the defense of the revolution itself. Segregated from the regular armed forces, it maintains its own army, air force, and navy, and is itself essentially a terrorist group.

While Iran's conventional military provides no threat to the American homeland, the organizations controlled by Iran do. Hezbollah has stated that they "have access to U.S. interests all over the world, even in the United States... The [Iranian] government and the leader [Khameni] are now preventing us from taking action, but as soon as they give us the green light no place will be safe for the Americans."

3. Iraq and Afghanistan

Iran has contributed greatly to the current chaos in Iraq and Afghanistan. In recent months, Iran has stepped up its support for the most radical

Iraqi militia groups, providing them with explosively formed penetrators (a form of roadside bomb capable of blasting through Humvee armor), armor-piercing bullets, and other weaponry. There is overwhelming evidence that the Revolutionary Guard is directing attacks on American forces, including the January 2007 attack in Karbala.

The direct attacks signal a shift in Iranian tactics, from indirect influencing of the Iraqi parliament to inflicting damage on the United States itself. This goal has now apparently superseded Iran's traditional Shia loyalties; Iranian bombs are now being found in Sunni-dominated areas of Iraq, and, in Afghanistan, where Iran has traditionally maintained a fierce hatred of the Taliban, it is now supplying weapons to that very group. Support of the Taliban, like support for Hamas, underscores the extent to which Iran will act to combat U.S. goals in the region.

4. Nuclear Weapons

Iran's secret nuclear weapons program was exposed six years ago. The program has existed in some form since at least the 1970s, but was thought

Anti-aircraft guns protect the Natanz nuclear facility

to have been abandoned. Yet, in 2002, the world discovered that Iran had a centrifuge cascade in Natanz, and a heavy-water plant in Arak. A heavy-water plant and centrifuge cascade are key components of a sustainable nuclear weapons program, enabling Iran to mine, refine, use, and dispose of its own nuclear material. Iran has continually prevented inspectors from visiting these and other crucial sites. Recently, suspicious construction activity has also been discovered at the Parchin missile-testing complex.

Considering Iran's capability of mining twenty-one tons of yellowcake uranium per year, there is no doubt that Iran possesses the raw material for a nuclear weapon. The CIA believes a viable Iranian bomb could be developed as early as 2010. Other intelligence agencies warn that Iran is much further along, and has already tested the trigger mechanisms needed to detonate a nuclear device. Mossad estimates Iran is as close as one year from nuclear armament.

5. Chemical and Biological Weapons

Iran is capable of producing both chemical and biological agents for battlefield use. Chemical-production factories are known to exist at more than a dozen sites around the country, each one capable of producing one thousand tons of nerve and blister agents suitable for warhead mounting. There is, too, a strong network of pharmaceutical companies and research scientists working on the creation of more deadly biological material, and it is believed that Iran has produced initial batches of usable biological agents.

6. Terrorist Proxies

Al Qaeda is desperate for a nuclear weapon to use against the United States. Hamas and Hezbollah are eager to bring the threat of nuclear annihilation to Israel. Iran could easily push such a weapon to any of these groups. Human transport has clear advantages over mechanical weapon-delivery devices, and would also provide the Iranian regime with some degree of deniability.

It is not unlikely that there are Hezbollah sleeper cells already within our country. With the majority of cargo entering the United States unscreened, a nuclear device could easily be smuggled in through a port. Such a weapon is likely to produce a thousand times more casualties and trauma than the World Trade Center attacks.

A nuclear weapon could be passed to one of these groups even against the wishes of the Iranian leadership—Iran's nuclear program is controlled not by its government, but by the Revolutionary Guard.

A CALIPHATE DISGUISED AS A REPUBLIC

To understand our options in Iran, one must understand the history and makeup of the Iranian government.

The modern Islamic Republic of Iran was built on anti-American-ism. America was the primary supporter of the shah, Iran's former ruler,

and instrumental in his seizure of power following the overthrow of the popular nationalist politician Mohammed Mossadeq in 1953.

The shah was exiled in 1979, and the charismatic cleric Ruhollah Khomeini took power. Khomeini was fiercely, almost maniacally anti-American, and injected this anti-Americanism into every facet of the revolution.

Ayatollah Ruhollah Khomeini

Hard-liners have been in control of the government since Khomeini's revolution. Shia Islam, the religion of the majority of Iranian citizens, places great trust in the high-est-ranking clerics. Historically they have been apolitical leaders, letting

the rulers rule. In forming the quasi-theocracy that rules Iran today, Khomeini leapt across that gap.

Constitutionally, Iran resembles a parliamentary democracy, but the concentration of power in religious leaders reduces elected officials to figureheads. The people elect a parliament, and a president who acts as head of state, appointing ministers and setting policy. But the unelected theocratic government exercises far more influence and control. The Expediency Coun-cil, made up of the clerical members of the Guardian

Mahmoud Ahmadinejad

Council, the heads of the three branches of government, and appointees of the supreme leader, is far more powerful than the parliament.

There are, too, institutions that exist partly within the realm of elected accountability and partly without it. The Guardian Council con-sists of six lawyers approved by parliament and six mullahs chosen by the supreme leader himself. The council has the power to suspend laws and veto candidates for parliament, which means that politicians opposed to the council are often prevented from running for office.

With this system in place, it is understandable that typical diplomacy has failed, since the institutions interacting with diplomats represent only a small portion of the actual government.

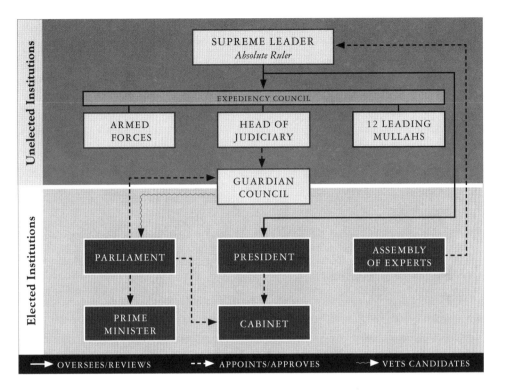

The current supreme leader, Ayatollah Khameni, has been zealous in promoting revolution. Iran's push toward nuclear weapons stems from his explicit orders. Khameni was nearly marginalized in 1999, following the election of the reformist president Mohammad Khatemi, but Khameni and other hard-liners responded to pressure against them by shuttering newspapers and assassinating Khatemi's deputies.

Iran's new president, Mahmoud Ahmadinejad, installed by the hard-liners in a rigged election, has promised to return Iran to the early days of the revolution, albeit with one new element—nuclear weaponry.

POSSIBLE MEASURES

1. Internal Options

There are no suitable internal options in Iran. Although Iran's population is dominated by the young—the median age is 25.8 years old, compared to 36.6 in the United States—and the young, on the whole, want greater freedom, the council and various military and police organizations maintain power over the populace. No significant policy change can be

One of several armed Iranian exile groups

expected. From an institutional viewpoint, the hard-liners remain firmly in control, and the council will continue to weed the electoral fields. Some opposition groups exist, but they are closely watched and effectively impotent.

Due to rampant anti-Americanism, any soft operations within the country would have to be carried out delicately. There is a general belief within Iran that the CIA has been toying with Iranian internal affairs. The population is sensitive to the slightest hint of foreign interference. Any covert team would have to be built from scratch, within the hypervigilant climate now in place.

2. Exile Groups

The national congress centered around Reza Pahlavi, heir to the shah, is the most effective of the Iranian exile groups. It has a charismatic leader and a built-in following. But failure of Ahmad Chalabi and the Iraqi National Congress (INC) bodes ill for this option. Most groups do not have a constituency within Iran, and many are actively reviled as traitors and hypocrites. Nevertheless, they do have firsthand cultural knowledge which could prove useful, and some still have networks within the country. These represent starting points for penetration by the CIA.

3. Negotiations

Iran has been under crippling sanctions ever since the revolution. Negotiations would involve setting aside these sanctions and allowing free trade, in exchange for regime change.

This strategy has been on the table since the Reagan administration. However, the current government of Iran is not predisposed to logical and well-defined benchmarks, nor even to ending the potential conflict peacefully and to the benefit of all involved.

4. Preemptive Strike

In 1981, Israeli warplanes dealt a crippling blow to Saddam Hussein's nuclear ambitions with a surgical strike on the Osirak reactor in Iraq. Based on excellent intelligence, Israel made the calculation that Iraq was on the verge of developing a nuclear weapon, and had to be stopped immediately.

Iran is at a similar breakthrough point in its own nuclear research. Destroying the program sites would forestall the problem, and reaffirm the United States's determination to keep nuclear weapons out of the hands of rogue regimes. Such an action would have quantifiable results, almost certainly leading to the suspension of other illicit-weapons programs across the world.

A strike would target the heavy-water plant at Arak along with the Isfahan Nuclear Technology Center, the Karaj research lab, the Natanz enrichment facility, the Parchin processing plant, the Bushehr reactors, the Ardakan fuel refinery, and the Anarak, Saghand, and Gchine uranium mines.

Additional planes could easily be used to hit missile and chemical-weapon plants at Isfahan, Damghan, Parchin, Karaj, and Qazvin, as well as barracks and command centers. A bombing campaign, if targeted properly, could be the catalyst for a full-scale revolt against the current regime.

5. Direct Action on Tehran

An initial mobile force moving into Tehran, bypassing other cities in favor of the fastest possible capture of senior leadership, followed by a much larger force tasked to establish a new government, could prove very effective. The Iranian population is much more unified than Iraq's, with a proud history and a single ethnic group. Civil war along sectarian lines is unlikely, and regional conflicts would resolve themselves quickly.

6. Large-Scale Invasion

A full-scale armed assault on the country, flanked appropriately with air and naval support, is entirely possible. It will, however, require overwhelming force and result in massive American casualties.

Serious plans for an invasion of Iran have been in development for five years. At least two operational plans exist to manage an invasion, and at least two conceptual plans have also been drawn up. The strategies vary in their demands for equipment, manpower, and strategic goals. Iran is a large country, the size of Alaska, with geographically difficult terrain.

7. The Khuzestan Gambit

Khuzestan, Iran's major oil-producing region, is blocked off from most of Iran's territory by the steep Zagros mountains, making it easily

Khuzestan and the Zagros Mountains

accessible to forces already in Iraq and on the Shatt al Arab waterway, and in range of U.S. carrier fleets. Only a few mountain passes connect Khuzestan to greater Iran. A lightning occupation of the territory, followed by a sealing-off of the passes, could strike a decisive blow against the regime.

Stripped of its income, Iran's government would be unable to maintain its security apparatus or the social-welfare programs that currently buy off the public. Additionally, without access to its refineries, the Iranian army would be unable to move. This strategy, if executed effectively, could limit casualties, though it could involve a significant time commitment.

CONCLUSION

Iran, in its present configuration, may be undeterrable. Rhetorically, it has already reverted to the hyperaggressive foreign policy it last displayed in the early '90s, and there is evidence that its actions will soon tend in the same direction. With a nuclear weapon, Iran would be freed from any fear of military reprisal. An attack on a nuclear-armed country would create grave risks; an attack on a nuclear-armed country with connections to terrorists able to place a nuclear weapon inside the United States could invite catastrophe.

A nuclear Iran would have free rein within the Middle East. An unencumbered Iran would likely attack Israel, foment Shia rebellions wherever the religious group formed a majority, threaten Saudi Arabia and Pakistan, and wage war against nations across the Persian Gulf. An Iranian bomb would also inevitably lead to nuclear proliferation within the region, as nations scrambled to neutralize the Iranian advantage. Solutions are still in reach, but time is short.

PAKISTAN

Pakistan, the world's only predominantly Muslim nuclear state, serves as a sanctuary and command center for terrorist groups and the nuclear black market. The nation's unstable dictatorial regime is too weak to confront the threatening entities it now shelters. It stands in danger of being overcome by extremist Islamic factions within the government, military, and populace at large. Without U.S. military action, Pakistan will, at best, continue to serve as a de-facto headquarters for terror. At worst, it will be remade as a jihadist nuclear state—an active provider of protection, foot soldiers, and nuclear weapons to al Qaeda and its brethren.

ABSTRACT

- Pakistan possesses an estimated eighty nuclear weapons, tested missiles with a 1,500-mile range, and a corrupt nuclear supply chain.

- The northern regions, especially North Waziristan and Kashmir, serve as a safe haven and staging ground for al Qaeda and the Taliban. It is likely that Osama bin Laden is now based there.

- Pervez Musharraf, Pakistan's military dictator and a stated supporter of the United States, is in danger of losing control of the country to an Islamofascist majority. Despite public posturing, he has done almost nothing to combat al Qaeda and the Taliban in Pakistan.

- Musharraf's government has ties to known terrorist groups and to the nuclear black market.

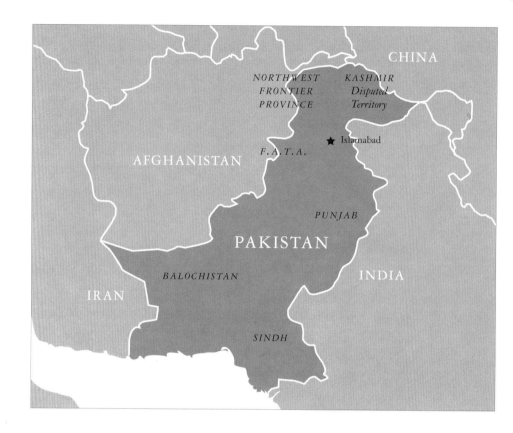

INTRODUCTION

The Islamic Republic of Pakistan sits on the coast of the Arabian Sea, sharing borders with Iran, Afghanistan, China, and India. It is the world's second-most-populous Muslim country (77 percent Sunni, 20 percent Shiite), made up of ethnic groups that include the Punjabi, Sindhi, Pashtun (Pathan), Baloch, and Muhajir, among others. Ethnic loyalties continue to divide the country, creating a constellation of far-flung strongholds that no central government has been able to control, let alone unify. Today, this has created a lawless zone that extremists have rushed to occupy, and a growing threat of nuclear weaponry falling into the hands of those who would use them against us.

Swift, strategic U.S. military action—combined with diplomatic maneuvers designed to keep Pakistani moderates in power—is essential to securing Afghanistan, preventing the emergence of a terrorist mini-state in Central Asia, and averting the nuclearization of the jihadist movement. Moreover, it would destroy the world's most active terrorist breeding ground, remove the top leadership of the Taliban and al Qaeda, and present the most likely chance of bringing Osama bin Laden to justice.

THREAT OVERVIEW

1. The Terrorist Mini-State of FATA

The mountainous regions of the Federally Administered Tribal Areas (FATA) run along the Pakistan-Afghanistan border, a lawless stretch that includes South and North Waziristan, as well as tribal land extending to the Mohmand and Bajaur areas. It is here that al Qaeda and the Pashtun Taliban are building a new terrorist state, recruiting new soldiers for jihad, integrating their leadership into the local Pashtun chiefdoms, and attracting a growing number of Islamic militant groups from around the world.

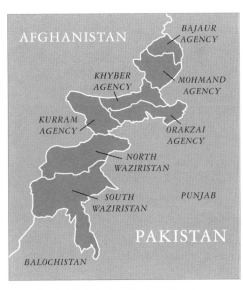

Detail of the Federally Administered Tribal Area

Osama bin Laden and his deputy Ayman al-Zawahri are believed to operate from this region; the presence of Taliban leaders Mullah Mohammad Omar and Jalaluddin Haqqani is also considered probable. Both the Taliban and al Qaeda use FATA as a base for guerilla warfare against U.S. soldiers in Afghanistan. The trail of 2007 terror plots in Germany and Denmark led to an active, organized, and fully operational al Qaeda outgrowth there. Other, more recent arrivals include fighters allied with Kashmir's Jaish-e-Mohammed (JEM), sometimes referred to as "the Punjabi Taliban." Al Qaeda provides the ideological center for these groups, along with financing and training.

The few efforts that have been made to impact the FATA enclave have failed. Ill-equipped Pakistani troops have suffered brutal losses in the

Tribal elders in the FATA region of Waziristan

face of bitter tribal resistance. On September 6, 2006, the Pakistani government agreed to a peace deal with the Taliban, which signed the cease-fire on behalf of "the Islamic Emirate of Waziristan." In the wake of this agreement, attacks on NATO forces in Afghanistan have tripled.

2. The Kashmir Powder Keg

The kingdom of Jammu and Kashmir lies to Pakistan's northeast, on the nation's border with India. It is claimed by both countries and control is split. Jihadist groups in Kashmir have long been used by as proxies by the Pakistani military, which provides them with extensive training and weapons. Between 1989 and 2002, eighty thousand people died in violence in the Kashmir region.

The kingdom represents an important incubator, thruway, and escape route for South and Central Asian terrorists. An estimated five thousand al Qaeda operatives have been spread throughout Kashmir; in June 2007, the Indian base of al Qaeda announced that it was also launching operations in the region. Many of the al Qaeda–linked militants who occupied Islamabad's Red Mosque lived and trained in Kashmir, and the terror nests are now becoming self-sufficient. The kingdom's Tora Bora–like terrain and ideologically vulnerable populace have stymied any attempts by the Pakistani government to police the region.

3. State Links to Terrorism

Terrorist activity has not been confined to the northern provinces. In 2002, the American consulate in Karachi was car-bombed, killing twelve Pakistanis and punching a hole in the fortified wall around the building. The torture and murder of American journalist Daniel Pearl provided

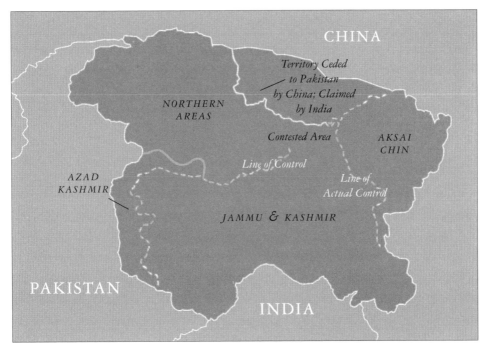

Detail of the disputed Kashmir region

further evidence that terrorists maintain a significant footing in Islamabad and Karachi.

More disturbing, however, are the established links between terror organizations and factions within the state apparatus of Pakistan. Elements within the Inter-Services Intelligence (ISI), Pakistan's intelligence agency, have been linked conclusively to Jaish-e-Mohammed, the organization responsible for Pearl's abduction and for several bombings in India and in Jammu and Kashmir over the last five years. The ISI operates almost independent of the Musharraf regime, and has long sponsored al Qaeda and the Taliban. With the help of a number of Musharraf's highest-ranking officials, the ISI has repeatedly allowed al Qaeda leadership to cross Pakistan's border in flight from U.S. forces in Afghanistan. There are reports that the ISI has also collected payments from al Qaeda in exchange for intelligence on CIA activities.

Symptomatic of the current situation was the arrest of al Qaeda's third-in-command, Khalid Sheikh Mohammed, along with another senior leader, in March 2003. They were discovered in the home of a Pakistani

Jamaat-e-Islami party member near Islamabad. In the weeks prior to their capture, both men were seen walking freely around the neighborhood, located not far from a large Pakistani army base. The Jamaat-e-Islami party, along with an Islamic political coalition called the United Front—linked to religious feeder schools for the Afghan jihad—command major blocks within the National Assembly.

4. Popular Support for Terrorists

A recent poll of the Pakistani populace reported substantially higher approval ratings for Osama bin Laden than for Musharraf or the American government. Sympathetic Pakistani civil-

Osama bin Laden

ians have aided and concealed terrorists, particularly where Pashtun groups are concentrated. The Taliban's version of sharia, a form of Islamic law that governs every aspect of daily life, is on the rise, prescribing the removal of women from public life and the establishment of Islamic religious schools called *madrassas*.

Unregulated madrassas provide a hermetic environment for ideological training. The schools offer free food and clothing to the most poverty-stricken denizens of Pakistan; in return, their students constitute a ready supply of aggressive supporters of violent anti-Americanism. Madrassa students are steeped in extremist propaganda, and made to understand that democracy and Islam are mutually exclusive. In some cases, madrassas are used as terrorist training camps; in others, they are essentially recruitment locations for al Qaeda, the Jammu and Kashmir Liberation Front (JKLF), and other groups. At least one of the perpetrators of the 2005 London subway bombings—fifty-two dead, seven hundred wounded—had links to a Pakistani madrassa.

5. A Precarious and Untrustworthy Dictatorship

Musharraf has stayed in power by currying favor with extremist Islamic parties. He survived six assassination attempts in 2002, two of which involved suicide bombers. Despite his stated alliance to Washington, terrorist activity has skyrocketed in Pakistan during his tenure. Musharraf has little popular support. Exiled leaders are returning to the country, and opposition figure Javed Hashmi, who was jailed for treason in 2004, has reemerged as a political threat.

President Pervez Musharraf

Musharraf's gambit is that the U.S. will continue to view supporting him as its only hedge against a jihadist power grab. As he is increasingly driven toward appeasement of extremists, however, it is clear that America must consider alternative courses of action.

6. The Muslim Bomb

In 2004, Dr. A. Q. Khan, the father of the Pakistani nuclear program, confessed to selling plans and material to North Korea, Iran, Saudi Arabia, Libya, and Malaysia. Musharraf pardoned Khan the next day. Israeli intelligence has intercepted communications between Iran and Pakistan that further implicate the president's office, suggesting that he directed the ISI and Khan to distribute nuclear technology to even the balance of power in the Muslim world. A nuclear inspection of Libya exposed raw materials based on Khan's designs, along with plans made by Khan for a half-ton nuclear bomb—too big for a warhead, but perfect for a large car.

Pakistan possesses between twenty-five and fifty highly enriched uranium nuclear warheads (HEUs). HEUs are rapidly convertible into much cruder nuclear weapons that can be fired from a variety of easily obtained devices, and require very little specialized technology or expertise to be immediately useful to terrorists. The presence of top terrorist leadership, the role of Musharraf's regime in nuclear king-making, and the real possibility of his loss of power to a Taliban-friendly regime, represent a perfect storm. Together, they make Pakistan, absent U.S. military action, the world's most likely place for a nuclear device to pass into terrorists' hands.

POSSIBLE MEASURES

1. Solidify and Validate a Moderate Regime

Extremist Islamic parties such as Jamaat-e-Islami and the United Front must be kept out of power. A power-sharing agreement with moderates—already being brokered with assistance from the U.K. and the U.N.—should be put in place prior to any U.S. military operations to stabilize the Musharraf regime.

Covert diplomatic operations could provide public opportunities for the Musharraf government to posture against selected U.S. activities, shoring up their support among nationalists. A withdrawal agreement offered by the United States in response to a Musharraf "ultimatum" after our operations have concluded—along with foreign aid packaged as reparations—should give the Musharraf regime credit for forceful sovereign assertion in the face of certain "unauthorized" U.S. actions. In return, the United States will provide substantial economic and military support to the regime.

2. FATA Search and Destroy

Reliable intelligence is essential for effective military strikes in Pakistan. The ISI must be viewed as a suspect source; direct alliances with local tribal leaders—along with aid packages and security—should be made, targeting Pashtun chiefs and others whose authority has been threatened or supplanted by the mullahs. New direct channels of intelligence must be created at any cost. Opportunities to feed al Qaeda bad information through the ISI prior to U.S. action should be explored.

At the same time, a new elite FATA unit must be created within the Pakistani army, one with proven loyalty to Musharraf. This unit could train secretly with U.S. attack forces, and, armed with actionable intelligence and air support on constant alert, enter with them from Afghanistan and attack terrorist camps in FATA, working with tribal leaders as they sweep back and forth across the border. For those terrorist forces that are not destroyed, all efforts would be made to drive them across the border into Afghanistan, where U.S. forces may operate with impunity. This would be a swift, wide pursuit with dual aims: the elimination of terrorist cells and the capture of bin Laden.

Although not a full-scale invasion, the sweep would require many units in order to be effective—highly trained forces with expertise in mountain fighting. Any strikes must be seen as micro-targeted operations which, while still distasteful to many Pakistanis, have become a familiar part of news from the north. As reports of wider operations began to hit the press, the Musharraf government would begin to publicly protest the United States's overstepping of its stated bounds. Operations, meanwhile, would continue unchecked. Once the major objectives are met, the United States would pull back its fighting units while escalating special-forces activities for cleanup and pursuit.

Pakistan is too large and complex a country to be stripped of its extremists militarily. However, these actions would destroy the top al Qaeda and Taliban leadership. They also represent the best and perhaps only chance for the United States to bring Osama bin Laden to justice. The result: Central Asia is purged of its most dangerous militants, and a more stable Pakistan can emerge, headed by pro-U.S. leaders with nationalist credibility.

3. Slamming the Kashmir Door

Kashmir presents a volatile challenge that no military force or ideological faction has managed to solve. Groups like the Jammu and Kashmir Liberation Front distribute Kalashnikovs to teenage soldiers; Islamic extremists fighting in the demilitarized zone will be difficult to control. Despite a belt of al Qaeda operatives spread through both Pakistani and Indian Kashmir, large-scale military action is out of the question.

However, simultaneous with the FATA strikes, small attack teams with air support could seek out and destroy terrorist strongholds here, targeting areas most likely to provide sanctuary for terrorists fleeing FATA. Chaotic conditions may make it easier for small units and special-operations teams to operate without attracting attention. In any event, targets must be carefully selected to keep Kashmir from erupting into full-blown civil war.

4. Contingency Airstrikes

The nightmare scenario, of course, involves Pakistan's nuclear arsenal falling into the hands of an Islamofascist regime. In this case, a quick strike to Pakistani stockpiles and military targets would prove highly effective. Targets could include the plutonium processing plant at Rawalpindi, uranium-enrichment facilities at Golra Sharif and Sihala, weapons facilities at Kahuta and Wah, and other supply-chain sites in Kundian, Chashma, Lakki, Issa Khel, Khushab, Lahore, Multan, and Dera Ghazi Khan. Although extreme, this measure would declaw the nuclear threat a terrorist-steered Pakistan would pose to the West.

CONCLUSION

For the United States, Pakistan has long represented a dangerous compromise. We have supported a moderate regime in the hope that Pakistan could be a partner in fighting terrorism and in keeping nuclear weapons out of the hands of extremists. That hope and that compromise have failed. The world's greatest terrorist stronghold only grows stronger, and fiercely anti-American Islamists are poised to take the reins of power.

Without action, Musharraf will fall. Our best and last chance to capture Osama bin Laden will disappear. The new government will use its nuclear deterrent to oppose any military action on Pakistani soil, while forming permissive agreements with al Qaeda and the Taliban. Pakistan's role as a terrorist command center and attack platform will thrive. Given time, terrorists will obtain a nuclear weapon in Pakistan and use it elsewhere, undeterred. New strategies must be explored without delay.

UZBEKISTAN

Uzbekistan has become a safe harbor for radical Islamic terrorist groups. It is now the most volatile nation in all of Central Asia, a serious risk to itself and the region, and a critical battleground in the global war on terror.

ABSTRACT

- Uzbekistan is a breeding ground and training center for radical Islamic groups, including the al Qaeda–linked Islamic Movement of Uzbekistan (IMU) and Hizb ut-Tahrir, which intends to establish an Islamic state in Uzbekistan.

- Widely condemned as one of the world's worst dictators, Uzbekistan's President Islam Karimov has remained in power for the last seventeen years through election fraud, the murder of his opponents, and the wholesale massacre of protesters. While his term ended in January 2007, to date he has taken no steps toward relinquishing power.

- Uzbekistan's location (between the Middle East, Russia, Pakistan, and China) makes it a crucial area to secure in the global fight against terror. However, U.S./Uzbekistan relations are at a boiling point. Karimov has evicted the United States from Kharshi-Khanabad airbase in Uzbekistan, a base that served as a vital staging ground in Operation Iraqi Freedom and in the delivery of humanitarian aid to northern Afghanistan.

- This impoverished state suffers from increasing curtailment of human rights and free speech, an ominous trend best exemplified by the 2005 massacre in Andijan of hundreds of protesters critical of President Karimov.

- Uzbekistan is plagued by drug trafficking and rampant narcoterrorism, and functions as a gateway for Taliban heroin trafficking from Afghanistan through Asia and into Europe.

INTRODUCTION

The Uzbekistan of today is a tinderbox of unrest and Islamic extremism. A mostly barren desert country about the size of California, it lies at the heart of Central Asia, where it shares borders with Afghanistan, Turkmenistan, Tajikistan, Kazakhstan, and Kyrgyzstan. Although the nation gained independence from the Soviet Union in 1991, Uzbekistan was for decades one of the Soviets' primary venues for the production and stockpiling of weapons and still houses Soviet-era weapons of mass destruction, as well as an ostensibly decommissioned large-scale chemical weapons production factory. President Karimov, pinned between a restive population and al Qaeda offshoots, can no longer be viewed as a steadfast guardian of this arsenal. Our actions must remove his ineffectual, destructive regime and replace it with a leader who will stabilize Uzbekistan, root out Islamic extremism in the Ferghana Valley, and secure Uzbekistan's weapons-grade fissile material and natural-gas holdings.

THREAT OVERVIEW

1. A Massive Stockpile of Weapons of Mass Destruction

Despite threat-reduction agreements and "loose nukes" management programs, Uzbekistan's WMDs are far from secure. Additionally, stocks of weapons-usable fissile material remain in Uzbekistan, some portion of which remains unaccounted for. Despite the efforts of the United States to improve accounting, the risks remain strikingly real.

President Islam Karimov

Rogue elements worldwide consider former Soviet states the easiest places to obtain WMDs, and Uzbekistan occupies a strategically significant territory—directly between nations possessing sizable WMD caches (Russia and the Ukraine) and nations actively seeking to build up their nuclear and chemical weapons capabilities (Iran, Syria, and others). Export and border-control systems in Uzbekistan lack funding, equipment, and trained personnel. There are already accounts of undocumented transfers of radioactive material out of the country.

2. The Tyranny of "President" Islam Karimov

Islam Abduganievich Karimov was appointed president of the Uzbek Soviet Socialist Republic by the Supreme Soviet on March 24, 1990. Using the Soviet tactics of torture, censorship, and rigged elections, as well as the slaughter of his own citizens, he has remained in power ever since.

In 1995, Karimov extended his term to 2000 via a widely criticized referendum. Karimov was "reelected" with 91.9 percent of the vote on January 9, 2000, in an election that the U.S. State Department has called "neither free nor fair... offer[ing] Uzbekistan's voters no true choice." The sole opposition candidate, Abdulhafiz Jalalov, admitted that he entered the race only to make it appear democratic, and that he voted for Karimov. The pattern continued on January 27, 2002, when Karimov "won" another referendum extending the length of presidential terms from five to seven years.

After the attacks of September 11, 2001, Uzbekistan was considered one of our strategic allies in the war on terror. Uzbekistan hosted eight

U.S. Soldiers patrol Kharshi Khanabad Air Base before its closing in 2005

hundred U.S. troops at the Karshi-Khanabad Air Base, also known as "K2," which provided one of the staging grounds for the 2001 invasion of Afghanistan. But Karimov expelled the United States from Uzbekistan in July 2005, after the Bush administration criticized his handling of a series of internal conflicts with Islamic extremists (detailed in the next section). Just

months before, on May 13, 2005, Karimov authorized the massacre of hundreds of mostly unarmed protesters in Andijan, Uzbekistan. He has

The massacre at Andijan

abandoned the war on terror, turning instead to indiscriminate actions against his own citizens and a retreat toward alliance with Russia. He also harbors conspiracy theories, accusing Western governments and major international media organizations like the BBC of helping to plan and carry out attempted uprisings.

It has become clear that Karimov's interest is only in retaining power, whatever the costs to his country. To this end, Karimov is willing to sacrifice good relations with the United States and the basic human rights of his own people. He has

wielded an iron fist against political opponents and dissidents for the last seventeen years, and will continue to do so for as long as he can.

3. Systemized Torture

Under Karimov, torture has flourished as a common practice in Uzbekistan's prisons. Indeed, it appears to be sanctioned as a standard interrogation method. In 2003, the U.K. *Guardian* reported that "there are more than 600 politically motivated arrests a year in Uzbekistan, and 6,500 political prisoners, some tortured to death… two prisoners were even boiled to death."

The U.S. Department of State and the organization Human Rights Watch have both released numerous reports documenting Uzbekistan's system of arbitrary arrest and torture, and its use of psychological pressure, beatings, the breaking of bones, electric shock, the shoving of needles under fingernails, suffocation, rape, immersion in boiling water, and other horrific acts. Although these methods are in violation of Uzbekistan's constitution and ratified international treaties, police and other authorities in Uzbekistan employ them with impunity.

This corruption and arbitrary violence have weakened the strength of the state and promoted a sense of lawlessness in the country. This lawlessness has, in turn, swelled the rising tide of terrorist groups by radicalizing Muslim Uzbeks.

4. Control of the Press

Censorship in Uzbekistan's media is reminiscent of the state's Soviet days, and effectively cuts off internal channels of opposition and nonviolent reform. Critical accounts of the Karimov administration are nearly impossible to find in Uzbek newspapers. Of the seven primary papers, five are either owned or run by the state; the other two are owned and run by Karimov's political party. The National Television and Radio Company is also controlled by the state, as are many radio stations and news agencies. Journalists have been imprisoned or "disappeared" for printing stories in the local and international media critical of Karimov's brutal actions. The populace is thus kept uninformed, disorganized, and prone to manipulation by the extremist fringe.

5. A Surging Islamic Terrorist Presence

Social reform has been an abysmal failure in Uzbekistan. Not only has

Karimov (an economist by trade) tacitly allowed poverty and corruption to spiral out of control, he has failed to provide the most basic social

IMU leader Tahir Yuldash

services, allowing what services were left over from the Soviet era to decay into disaster. In the Ferghana Valley region, the worsening poverty has been echoed by a second trend—rising extremism.

The Islamic Movement of Uzbekistan and Hizb ut-Tahrir, both affiliated with al Qaeda and the Taliban, have grown in size and become increasingly active regionally. Both groups have a twofold agenda: eliminating the secular regime of President Karimov, and assisting the international war against the United States led by al Qaeda, the Taliban, and Osama bin Laden. Al Qaeda considers Uzbekistan to be of strategic value as a conduit for the flow of arms and fighters, and of great cultural value because of its rich Islamic history. Uzbekistan's proximity to Afghanistan makes it particularly important in the war on terror.

The IMU and Hizb ut-Tahrir are part of a larger network of Islamic extremist organizations. Intelligence indicates that the Taliban aided the IMU in the 1990s by harboring militants and providing training camps in Afghanistan. In addition, the IMU, with an active membership suspected to number in the thousands, has received direct financial assistance from al Qaeda. In 2001, information about the then-upcoming attacks on the World Trade Center was obtained from an intercepted communication between al Qaeda and one of the IMU's leaders, Tahir Yuldash. At the time, Yuldash was hiding in Afghanistan with bin Laden.

Insurgents and trainees have, since the early 1990s, streamed back and forth across the Uzbek-Afghan border. Former IMU leader Juma Namangani, killed in the early days of Operation Enduring Freedom, spent his last months training al Qaeda insurgents in northern Afghanistan, where he established an IMU camp. In 2000, he set up "a forward base of operations" in Batken, Kyrgyzstan, and in December of that year, Namangani moved three hundred well-armed guerillas to a new camp location in Tajikistan. Intelligence sources indicate Namangani was even appointed as a "deputy" to bin Laden sometime in 2001. In May 1999, Tahir Yuldash obtained permission from the Taliban to establish another IMU camp in northern Afghanistan, a camp designed to train insurgents and route arms and information between Afghanistan and Uzbekistan.

In recent years, IMU attacks have focused on the Uzbek-Kyrgyz border, indicating the IMU's ambition to ignite a broader, regional conflict. Increasingly, IMU operatives have conducted attacks more openly, withdrawing to villages and camouflaging themselves as locals rather than, as before, retreating to the Ferghana Valley or the surrounding mountains. They are, in short, becoming bolder.

Within the next five years, terrorist organizations like the IMU and Hizb ut-Tahrir will have developed an alarming strength and capacity both inside Uzbekistan and regionally. This presents two immediate threats to our interests:

1) Islamic extremists will gain enough power to overthrow the Karimov regime and, in its place, establish a violent Islamic state similar to Afghanistan under the Taliban. This would represent not only a giant step backward for the region but a grave danger to our soldiers in Iraq and Afghanistan. Such an event would also lead to widespread violence, if not civil war, within Uzbekistan.

2) Even if a coup does not occur, swollen ranks of the IMU and Hizb ut-Tahrir would mean a dramatically increased flow of arms and terrorist expertise between Uzbekistan and Afghanistan. Some of these armed insurgents will kill Americans on the Afghan front. Others, trained by Uzbeks in either Afghanistan or Uzbekistan, will undoubtedly end up in Iraq, where they will attack our soldiers and innocent Iraqis. And some will soon arrive in Europe and the United States.

As long as these terrorist operations are allowed to expand in Uzbekistan, our troops and interests are imperiled.

6. Rampant Narcoterrorism

Uzbekistan is a primary transit country for opiates originating in Afghanistan. Well-established trade routes facilitate the movement of these drugs to Russia and Europe, and then to the rest of the world. There is a growing market for a variety of drugs from Afghanistan and consequently a growing problem with drug addiction, drug smuggling, and the spread of HIV/AIDS (via heroin use).

Despite a number of agreements committing Uzbekistan to fight drug trafficking more forcefully, the country has done little. Since neighboring Turkmenistan clamped shut its borders, cutting off imports and exports of all kinds, Uzbekistan has become the preferred transit route through Central Asia. The United Nations Office on Drugs and Crime (UNODC) released a report in August 2007 anointing Afghanistan as "practically the exclusive supplier of the world's deadliest drug (93% of the global opiates market)." The UNODC report goes on to say that "opium cultivation in Afghanistan is now closely linked to insurgency" and that the Taliban is "extract[ing] from the drug economy resources for arms, logistics and militia pay." Uzbekistan is, by extension, an enabler of the ongoing conflict across its border.

The Taliban-linked IMU also uses drug trafficking as a means of financing its terrorist operations. IMU leaders provide routine and extensive armed cover for drug transports through northern Afghanistan and the Ferghana Valley. The alarming increase in Afghanistan territory cultivated for opium (now up to 193,000 hectares), combined with the Taliban's opium trafficking through Uzbekistan, demonstrates the urgent need for the United States to take decisive action.

POSSIBLE MEASURES

It should be noted that the Uzbek military is underfunded and ill-equipped; the army and air force combined have only forty thousand soldiers. Most Uzbek military equipment is left over from the Soviet era and poorly maintained. Unlike other former Soviet states, which have allowed Russian guards to patrol within or on their borders, Uzbekistan has refused Moscow's assistance. Attacking Uzbekistan via an air strike targeting the hot sites in the Ferghana Valley would be quite easy. However, it is uncertain how effective such a measure would be against less centralized militant forces and terrorist cells. A more comprehensive strategy is necessary.

1. Economic Sanctions

The United States must rally the international community to cut off all trade and financial activity with Uzbekistan. These sanctions will bring the Uzbek economy to a halt, pressuring Karimov's already beleaguered government into impotence. Sanctions will make it impossible for Karimov to pay his troops, his air-force personnel, and his own officials. This sealing-off of finances will also, no doubt, place a strain on the operations of the IMU and other terrorist groups.

2. Fomentation of a Popular Uprising

Like the United States–backed Color Revolutions in Eastern Europe and Central Asia, and more recent post-Soviet "democracy movements" in Serbia, Georgia, and Kyrgyzstan, a well-supported popular revolt against the Karimov dictatorship may well prove to be effective, particularly if the central government is already weakened by sanctions. This would require training and encouragement of the populace in modern methods of mass resistance, and the rallying of massive workers' strikes through large media campaigns and word of mouth. Uzbekistan's infrastructure would be crippled until Karimov resigned.

3. Air Strikes

Using already-established U.S. bases in neighboring nations, our Air Force could quickly strike Uzbekistan. The necessary staging facilities, either owned and operated by the United States or available for our use, are already in place in the Ukraine, Afghanistan, Israel, Turkey, and within the borders of other willing NATO allies, especially those in Eastern Europe.

These air strikes would target military assets—anti-aircraft installations, barracks, hangars, training camps, bases, and bunkers—primarily

Uzbek soldiers

those located along the Uzbek border and around Tashkent, the capital city. A second wave of strikes against outlying military locations, namely in and around Bukhara, Urgench, Samarkand, and Nukus, would commence shortly after. In recognition of Uzbekistan's WMD capabilities, these air strikes would avoid chemical and nuclear weapons facilities, which would be dismantled after the country has been secured. This second wave would also concentrate firepower on the Ferghana Valley region, delivering a paralyzing blow to important highways, train stations, and airports, and destroying the terrorist training facilities of the Islamic Movement of Uzbekistan.

If these first waves of air strikes did not inspire surrender, our air force would begin a third round, meant to cripple the country's economic capabilities. These attacks would target docks on the Aral Sea, supply depots, factories, and various government buildings. The aerial siege would block all commercial and civilian traffic and trade into or out of Uzbekistan not already halted by the economic sanctions. At the same time, the destruction of border roads into Afghanistan would help cut off the funding of narcoterrorism and the importation of weapons into the Ferghana Valley.

CONCLUSION

The situation in Uzbekistan—WMD stockpiles and manufacturing facilities, an increasingly repressed and thus increasingly radicalized populace, a tradition of ineffectiveness toward narcoterrorism and Islamic terrorism—raises the specter of several deleterious events. At any point in the near future, terrorists, radicalized Islamic sects, or shadow elements from countries like North Korea or Iran could easily obtain "loose nukes" from Uzbekistan. Barring that, they could use Uzbekistan as an easy traffic conduit, shipping deadly weapons out of the region and into the hands of terrorist operators.

Such an occurrence would be catastrophic. Uzbekistan, used as a conduit or supplier by terrorists, might prove the crucial link in a chain leading to a major terrorist attack on the scale of September 11, 2001. Now is the time for the United States to step forward and secure this region, before the overthrow of Karimov, or further massacres, cast Uzbekistan into chaos.

VENEZUELA

Flush with oil revenue, Venezuelan President Hugo Chavez is an unstable and increasingly dictatorial leader intent on throwing his nation and the surrounding region into chaos. Unless dealt with, he will destabilize U.S. strategic positions around the globe.

ABSTRACT

- Chavez has emerged as the leading proponent of "Bolivarism," a culturally rooted brand of socialism that seeks to subsume the nations of Central and South America into an ideologically aligned, independent power bloc, with Venezuela at its center.

- Venezuela has opened its borders to terrorist groups, and is forming relationships with anti-American nations, as well as with non-state terrorist organizations.

- These same borders are increasingly porous to human traffickers who subsist on the sexual exploitation of women and children.

- Venezuela's permissive stance toward drug-trafficking narcoterrorist organizations effectively funnels revenue to and from them.

- Chavez's military spending, and possible nuclear goals, raise the risk of assaults on neighboring nations, and on the United States itself.

INTRODUCTION

Just one thousand miles south of Florida, Venezuela is located on the northern coast of South America, bordering Brazil, Guyana, and Colombia. Its president, Hugo Chavez, is a deeply religious (and decidedly superstitious) man who believes himself to be the reincarnation of Ezequiel Zamora, a Robert E. Lee–esque figure from Venezuela's Federal War in the mid-1800s. He also considers himself the ideological descendant of Simón Bolívar, the South American war hero who is credited with helping to liberate Venezuela, among other countries. Chavez is so enamored of Bolívar that he keeps an empty chair in his office and meeting rooms for Bolívar's ghost.

This belies his true standing as a corrupt strongman who has squandered his nation's natural resources and misled its electorate. Today, Chavez holds visions of the impending collapse of the U.S. economic system, and is determined to prepare his country for this downfall. He asserts that he will help build a "Bolivarian axis" in Latin America, linking Venezuela to Cuba, Argentina, and Brazil in order to to curb U.S. influence in the region. With this increasingly belligerent anti-American rhetoric, Chavez has managed to convince Venezuelans that they must prepare to defend themselves against a U.S. threat. In July of 2006, he signed a military cooperation agreement with Belarus for more than $1 billion in arms deals.

THREAT OVERVIEW

1. Narcoterrorism

It is widely acknowledged that Venezuela represents a safe haven and transit corridor for drugs and arms. In 2005, Hugo Chavez formally severed all ties with the U.S. Drug Enforcement Administration, calling it a "drug cartel." Up to two hundred tons of cocaine (one-quarter of the global supply) are smuggled through Venezuelan borders each year; drug traffickers in the region refer to Venezuela as "a gateway to heaven."

Cocaine seized by Canadian police, part of 300 kg arriving from Port of La Guaira in Venezuela

In addition to providing a transit route for narcotics, Venezuela has also become a shelter for drug lords. Various narcoterrorist groups—including Colombian organizations such as Fuerzas Armadas Revolucionarias de Colombia (FARC) and the Ejército de Liberación Nacional de Colombia (ELN)—have a significant presence in Venezuela. Autodefensas Unidas de Colombia (AUC), a right-wing paramilitary counterrevolutionary force responsible for more deaths than any other group in the region, has claimed that 70 percent of its revenue comes from drug-related activities, no doubt conducted with the assistance of Venezuelan authorities. Smugglers often load cocaine onto airplanes in plain sight, at public commercial airports.

Venezuela's drug trade has deadly repercussions around the world. The Taliban raises a significant portion of its revenues from drug sales, with Venezuela serving as a major port for opium brought in from Afghanistan and other parts of the Middle East.

2. Iran's Trojan Horse

Chavez's Venezuela has, especially in recent years, developed an extensive and alarming web of connections to both terrorist organizations and terrorist-friendly nations. Beyond symbolic actions like visiting Hussein's Iraq and Qaddafi's Libya, Chavez has engaged in clandestine support for a range of terrorist outfits in South America and the Middle East and positioned Venezuela among an infamous group of nations aiding, assisting, and even speaking out in favor of entities that commit heinously violent crimes.

Hugo Chavez and Mahmoud Ahmadinejad

At the same time, Chavez continues to berate U.S. efforts to effect democratic reform in Iraq and Afghanistan, and to position his politics squarely against the United States's war on terror. Consequently, Venezuela has become the gravest threat to U.S. security interests in the western hemisphere.

On February 15, 2006, Nicolás Maduro, the head of the Venezuelan parliament, stood side by side with the speaker of the Iranian Parliament, Gholam Ali Haddad Adel, and said, "From our souls, we feel that our two nations are brothers and that together with other peoples we are carrying the flag of dignity and sovereignty." In the fall of that year, Iranian president Mahmoud Ahmadinejad visited Caracas and declared that the two nations have "common thinking, common interests." The Chavez government has established a number of agreements with Iran, ranging from investment pacts to cultural exchanges to pledges of support against military aggression—ostensibly as a warning to the United States. When Ahmadinejad came to Venezuela, he was welcomed as a hero with full military honors.

3. A Gateway for Rogue Nations and Dangerous Non-State Actors

In August 2006, Chavez visited Syria, proclaiming that he and the Syrian government are united in opposition to the United States. Chavez's alliance with Syria was deepened when he compared Israel's attacks on Hezbollah militants to the Holocaust and withdrew Venezuela's ambassador to Israel.

North Korea has also courted Venezuela, and Chavez has responded, offering stronger economic and political ties to the communist dictatorship. In 2005, the vice president of North Korea's parliament, Yang Hyong Sop, applauded Chavez's government for helping bring about "important achievements in the process of constructing twenty-first-century socialism" in Venezuela. In return, Chavez has announced that he will continue to strengthen "strategic alliances" with Pyongyang, and openly supports North Korea's development of its missile program.

Even more alarming than Venezuela's partnerships with rogue nations is its cooperation with non-state terrorist organizations like Hamas and Hezbollah, both of which operate freely on Isla de Margarita, a Venezuelan island in the Caribbean. From Isla de Margarita, Hezbollah runs an Arabic-language propaganda radio station, the only one of its kind in the Western Hemisphere. Hezbollah Venezuela also maintains a website, complete with a list of violent objectives and a logo featuring a fist clenching a rifle.

4. Rapid Armament and Ambitious Nuclear Goals

With its arms spending ballooning to $4.3 billion since 2005, Venezuela has become Latin America's largest weapons buyer. By comparison, in the same year Pakistan spent $3 billion on its military, and Iran spent $1.7 billion. Chavez has urged his soldiers to prepare for a "guerilla-style war" against the United States, and within his standing army of 82,300 troops he has established a special force of 20,000 for internal operations.

Last year, Venezuela became Moscow's fifth-largest arms client. Already, Chavez has purchased one hundred thousand Kalashnikov AK-103 rifles, twenty-four Su-30 Sukhoi fighter jets, and fifty-three Russian helicopters; there have been reports that he is seeking to obtain five

Project 636 Kilo-class diesel-electric submarines. Naval analysts agree that the acquisition represents an indisputable threat to the United States and its interests.

An Su-30 Sukhoi fighter jet

Chavez, defending Iran's right to pursue a nuclear program—he voted against referring Iran to the U.N. Security Council for its actions—has said that it might be a good idea for Venezuela eventually to do so itself. His outspoken advocacy for the nuclear programs of Iran and North Korea likely has a quid pro quo component, as Chavez harbors ambitions that these programs can in due course funnel nuclear capabilities to his own country.

5. Human Trafficking

Chavez permits Venezuela to act as a source, transit point, and destination for women and children trafficked for the purposes of commercial sexual exploitation and forced labor. Human trafficking—a kind of modern-day slavery—is a global health risk and a major source of income for organized crime. Women and children from Brazil, Colombia, Peru, Ecuador, the Dominican Republic, and the People's Republic of China are trafficked to and through Venezuela. The country does not comply with the minimum standards for the elimination of trafficking, and has made no significant efforts to do so. Chavez has yet to pass laws consistent with international standards, or to show any credible effort to investigate and prosecute trafficking offenses.

A STRONGMAN PRESIDENT

Chavez was elected in 1998, on a platform promising complete governmental restructuring and a rewritten constitution. His new constitution was drafted and approved by popular referendum, and took effect in December 1999, radically concentrating Chavez's power. More recent reforms have put the state's major institutions under his control: the judiciary, the electoral council, the armed forces, and, against the public's wishes, the state-owned oil company Petróleos de Venezuela (PDVSA). He was re-elected in December 2006.

Chavez was born into poverty in rural Venezuela. He joined the army in 1971 as a seventeen-year-old officer cadet and was influenced by its prevailing left-wing revolutionary ideas. He participated in socialist movements while earning an education through the military,

Hugo Chavez delivers a speech in Brazil in 2005

eventually helping to form the Revolutionary Bolivarian Movement–200 (MBR–200). From the beginning, this project was pro-Cuban, and combined the influences of the military left with Venezuelan nationalism. As he ascended the ranks, Chavez began to believe that civilian politicians are necessarily corrupt, and has held fast to this notion throughout his rise to power.

In 2002, public opposition to Chavez soared when he attempted to commandeer PDVSA. The widely publicized event caused government and military officials to rally against Chavez's undemocratic and authoritarian practices. Public opposition mobilized a civilian protest in which an estimated four hundred thousand to six hundred thousand Venezuelans marched through downtown Caracas to demand Chavez's resignation.

During the protest, dozens of shots were fired into the crowd by government forces, resulting in as many as two dozen deaths and more than one hundred injuries. Reporter Jorge Tortoza was shot dead while carrying a camera and wearing a vest clearly identifying him as a member of the press. Witnesses said Tortoza was deliberately targeted by a military sniper firing from the roof of City Hall.

In the wake of the demonstration, military leaders asked the president to leave office. Chavez allegedly resigned and was arrested, at which point Pedro Carmona, the leader of a Venezuelan business owners' association, became interim president. However, a small group of right-wing military leaders took control of the government, and the military high command restored Chavez to power. Almost immediately, Chavez began to purge his political opponents.

POSSIBLE MEASURES

1. Sanctions and Blockades

Sanctions would make Venezuela ineligible for many types of foreign investment, without interrupting humanitarian, counter-narcotics, and certain other types of assistance. It would both heighten the economic woes of the Chavez regime and increase the domestic pressure for change.

We can further isolate Venezuela by enacting a full naval blockade. Such a blockade would cut off Venezuela's coastline, weakening the regime and hindering its ability to interact with our enemies. Naval cruisers, carriers, and submarines would enter Venezuelan waters (perhaps as close as five miles out), crushing Venezuelan shipping and water transit until Chavez steps down.

Chavez fears such a blockade, and has been buying submarines from Russia and Eastern Europe in order to prepare for this possibility. He knows, in short, his vulnerability.

2. Covert Support for a Military Takeover

While an economic and infrastructural blockade occupies the public's imagination, the CIA must make contact with officers and soldiers in the Venezuelan military sympathetic to regime change. Unrest is rampant in the military—high-ranking officials are disgruntled with Chavez's oppressive socialist agenda, and the near-coup of April 2002 revealed the depth of unease in all quarters when, from top to bottom, military officials refused to follow Chavez's orders. The CIA would seek out and support— in utter secrecy—military officials to lead a coup d'état as well as soldiers eager for democracy who are willing to carry out such a coup. The CIA can provide funding, training, intelligence, and strategy. In this way, regime change—on the surface—will be the product of internal forces.

Support for Chavez's revolution also remains hollow in the oil industry and the bureaucracy—two segments of Venezuelan society ripe for oppositional activity. From here would come the public support for a military coup, in the form of campaigns devoted to exposing the bone-chilling record of Chavez's regime.

3. Bolstering Our Military Presence in Surrounding Countries

In any scenario, Colombia and Peru offer promising contingencies. While it is preferable that regime change be instigated by forces inside Venezuela, it is not improbable that new leaders would welcome immediate armed assistance from the United States to maintain order and stabilize the new regime during its infancy. Troops and equipment could be directed to current (and, if necessary, expanded) military positions throughout Colombia and Peru, as both nations are amenable to a U.S. military presence. Should our armed involvement become necessary—either through direct invitation by coup leaders, or in the event that a coup alone does not succeed—we would be in a position to act.

4. Multilateral Action through the Organization of American States

Chavez's violent revolutionary fomentation in the region has alarmed many neighboring nations, most of whom are active members in the Organization of American States (OAS)—they fear where Chavez will go once he feels he has the power and authority to expand the Revolutionary Bolivarian Movement's totalitarian mandate. Guyana, for instance, a country that shares Venezuela's eastern border, has expressed deep dread of the threat Venezuela poses to at least a third of its territory. Colombia's government, meanwhile, continues to denounce Venezuela's support for the destructive and violent FARC. Even Brazil, which has a left-wing president who publicly expresses some appreciation for Chavez's policies, considers him a significant danger to its national interests. The OAS may thus serve an important role, facilitating enforcement of sanctions, support for internal opposition, and, if necessary, direct invasion and containment of the Venezuelan threat.

OAS support for any ground invasion would be essential, especially if Chavez's regime proves more resilient than expected. Military action bolstered by the credibility and resources of the OAS would be decisive, bloodless, and infinitely more expeditious than unilateral measures.

CONCLUSION

In 1830, Simón Bolívar wrote, "America is ungovernable... Those who serve a revolution plough the sea." Though he was speaking of what he viewed as the collapse of the United States's own revolutionary experiment, he might well have been describing modern-day Venezuela. In Bolívar's name, Hugo Chavez has recklessly lowered Venezuela into the muck of tyranny and terrorism. His Revolutionary Bolivarian Movement purports to provide Venezuelans with freedom, opportunity, and adequate resources. The reality, however, does not reflect the ideal. The sad truth, revealed by Chavez's failure to combat narcoterrorists like FARC and Hezbollah, and by his affections for renegade states like Iran and Syria, is that Bolivarianism is a utopian dream, unattainable and misguided. In its place, Chavez has erected an increasingly threatening regional flashpoint, brutal to its own people and inviting to bad actors of all stripes, propped up by a level of military spending that can only tip into warlike behavior toward Venezuela's neighbors. We must recognize this dangerous fantasy for what it is.

SYRIA

The Syrian Arab Republic is a state sponsor of global terrorism, a base of operations for Hamas, Palistinian Islamic Jihad, and Fatah al-Islam, and a source of weaponry for Hezbollah. The country serves as a willing conduit for the movement of Iranian arms into Lebanon and of radical jihadists into Iraq, and is known to have stockpiled chemical and biological weapons. It has spent the last two decades attempting to obtain nuclear weaponry, and last year came closer to that goal than ever before.

ABSTRACT

- Syria's support for terrorist groups with international reach poses a direct threat to U.S. interests. Hezbollah, among other organizations, is funded and trained by Syria and supported by the Syrian military.

- Syria's six-hundred-kilometer border with Iraq is a virtual superhighway for jihadists bent on attacking our soldiers.

- Besides producing chemical and biological weapons, Syria has in recent years shown increased interest in nuclear technology. It has brought in North Korean engineers, contacted members of the A. Q. Khan network, and begun to assemble the necessary facilities. This activity threatens to put nuclear weapons within short range of U.S. forces in Iraq, Israeli population centers, Turkey, and much of Europe.

- Syria plays a destabilizing role in the Middle East. It has long interfered in Lebanon's internal affairs, and has participated in three wars against Israel. A U.N. tribunal has indicted top Syrian officials for the 2005 assassination of former Lebanese prime minister Rafik Hariri.

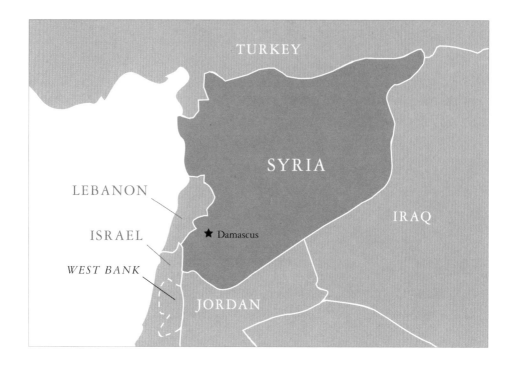

- The ruthless Assad dynasty has, since 1970, stifled democracy with a program of mass detentions, torture, "disappearing" of political opponents, and near-total elimination of civil liberties.

- The United States has made extraordinary efforts to conduct diplomacy with the Assad regime, including two recent congressional delegations and talks between senior officials. But Syria remains unwilling to alter its belligerent posture or to voluntarily control its border with Iraq.

INTRODUCTION

President Bashar al-Assad is the head of the ruling Ba'ath party, which is guaranteed primacy in the nation's constitution; his father, Hafez al-Assad, ruled the country from 1970 to 2000. After the death of Hafez, Bashar ran for president in a sham election in which he took 97 percent of the vote. A brutal crackdown on free speech and opposition elements soon began. Today, Bashar's regime has one of the worst human-rights records in the Arab world.

Syria has been involved in every major regional conflict of the past forty years. It serves as a major obstacle to a peaceful Middle East, and remains a serious threat to U.S. forces and allies in the region. Syria's alliance with Iran, its support for Hezbollah, Hamas, and al Qaeda in Iraq, and its unwillingness to take even the most basic measures to halt the flow of insurgents crossing into Iraq collectively suggest a threat too great to be left to the soft measures and shaky results of diplomacy.

THREAT OVERVIEW

1. The Porous Border

Without closing the Syrian border to insurgents, America will never be able to peacefully complete its work in Iraq. Syria is the insertion point for radical jihadists entering Iraq, and Syrians make up much of the mercenary insurgency now plaguing that country. These non-Iraqi radicals place no value on life or freedom, report directly or indirectly to al Qaeda, and have no interest in peace or negotiations, as they expect an Islamic dictatorship to rise from the ashes of the chaos they aim to create. Coalition forces and U.S. diplomats have repeatedly requested that Syria take measures to halt the flow of insurgents and funds, but the problem has not abated.

U.S. soldiers detain a Syrian fighter en route to Iraq

Syria also provides a haven for former Iraqi Ba'athists now coordinating insurgent activities from the safety of their new sponsor state. Major terrorist attacks in Iraq have been traced back to a Syrian bomb factory. Captured insurgents have admitted to receiving their training at camps in western Syria. In 2003, wiretaps painted a detailed picture of Syria's central role in the movement of recruits and money between Europe and Iraq, often through Damascus International Airport. Despite the ease of policing this travel hub, and international condemnation for its failure to do so, the Syrian government has done nothing.

The ease of travel between Syria and Iraq is such that insurgents from other countries that also border Iraq frequently travel through Syria anyway. Extremists recruited from across the Middle East, North Africa, and Europe customarily meet their handlers in Syria, where they are trained to conduct high-visibility, mass-casualty suicide attacks on coalition forces and civilian population centers. Between 80 and 90 percent of suicide attacks in Iraq are perpetrated by such foreign fighters.

2. State Sponsorship of Terrorism and Regional Unrest

Syria, like Iran, provides direct support for Hezbollah, the most well-armed and well-coordinated non-state military organization in the

world. Hezbollah was responsible for the 1983 Beirut barracks bombing in which 241 American servicemen were killed, and has expressed a willingness and ability to attack American interests across the globe. Despite this, Syria maintains a pipeline for arms shipments from Iran to Hezbollah, and allows Hezbollah agents to move unchecked across its border with Lebanon.

Members of Fatah al-Islam clash with Lebanese police

Other terrorist groups, including Palestinian Islamic Jihad and Hamas, are headquartered in Damascus and protected by the Syrian government. Syrian intelligence agencies provide support and weapons to Fatah al-Islam, an al Qaeda affiliate in northern Lebanon whose founder, Shaker al-Absi, was involved in the 2002 assassination of U.S. diplomat Laurence Foley in Jordan. Fatah al-Islam's more recent clashes with Lebanese police have led to the displacement of approximately forty thousand people.

3. Support for al Qaeda

Al Qaeda in Iraq is dependent for its survival on funding it receives from the global al Qaeda network, the majority of which flows through Syria. Syrian al Qaeda cells include Jund al Sham, whose philosophy calls for the forcible annexation of Lebanon and Israel into "Greater

Syria." The Syrian Abu al-Ghadiyah's terrorist cell shares responsibility for some of the most spectacular atrocities committed by al Qaeda in Iraq, including the mosque bombing in Samarra and the suicide bombing of the United Nations headquarters. Even al Qaeda's twenty-four-hour television station, al Zawraa, is based in Syria, broadcasting calls for violence against Americans.

4. Partnership with Iran

The Syria-Iran alliance constitutes a major, long-term threat. It is not an exaggeration to describe Hezbollah as a joint Syrian-Iranian terrorist project, and Syrian cooperation is crucial to Iran's arms shipments to its proxy groups. With Syrian approval, Iran's Revolutionary Guard runs a training camp for Hezbollah fighters in Lebanon's Beqaa Valley.

With the bulwark of Saddam Hussein removed, Syria and Iran clearly see an opportunity to control the region. Their shared goal is the establishment of a nuclear-armed axis stretching from the Persian Gulf to the Mediterranean Sea.

5. Conventional Forces and Weapons of Mass Destruction

The Assad regime is believed to possess more than a thousand Scud B and C missiles with ranges of up to six hundred kilometers. It has also developed Korean No-Dong/Scud-D missiles with much greater range, thanks to North Korean assistance. Missiles and launchers are stored in well-fortified facilities in the mountains near Damascus and the Palmyra region, and can be quickly moved to forward positions.

A Scud tactical ballistic missile

Over the past decade, the Assad regime has armed hundreds of these missiles with sarin and tabun warheads, as well as cluster warheads with VX bomblets. Having never ratified the 1972 Biological and Toxin Weapons Convention, Syria has now begun to weaponize anthrax, botulinum, and ricin for use with incendiary bombs and Scud warheads. The CIA estimates that Syria's biological warheads have the lethality of a fifty- to one-hundred-kiloton nuclear weapon.

But Syria is not satisfied with this equivalency. Since the early 1990s, it has acquired nuclear technology from China and North Korea, and has sought to buy thousands of tons of yellowcake uranium from Namibia. It is reported that as North Korea scales down its nuclear program, it has begun to transport much of its stockpiled material to Syria, along with experienced engineers. On September 6, 2007, with American approval, Israeli warplanes bombed Dayr az Zwar, a nuclear facility in northern Syria built with North Korean assistance. Syria's relatively muted response to the attack suggests it is not eager for a U.N. investigation of the site, or for speculation about other such locations. While Syria's nuclear program does not appear to be as advanced as Iran's, it is clearly trying to close the gap.

HUMAN RIGHTS VIOLATIONS

1. Citizens' Rights

Syria has operated under a state of emergency since 1963, with severe limitations on freedom of expression, association, and assembly. Women's rights have been abrogated. The Syrian Ba'ath party stifles dissent through mass detentions, outlawing of opposition groups, and widespread torture by security agencies. Syria is, essentially, a police state, where imprisonment without trial or access to medical care is common. Amnesty International and other human rights groups estimate that at least seventeen thousand political activists and opponents of the regime have been "disappeared" in recent years.

2. The Media

All media is controlled by the state. Criticism of the president and his family is banned, and foreign reportage is tightly censored. The Syrian

Telecommunications Establishment (STE), the country's only Internet service provider, blocks access to opposition sites.

3. Mistreatment of Minorities

Syria's oppression of its Kurdish minority is extreme. Concentrated in the mountainous region north and east of Aleppo, Kurds have been prohibited from using the Kurdish language or registering children with Kurdish names, refused passports, and deprived of the right to vote. They are forced to carry identity cards, cannot marry Syrian citizens, and are effectively barred from employment outside of Kurdish enclaves. An estimated 65,000 unregistered Kurds are barred from schools and public services and denied legal protections.

4. Human Trafficking

According to a recent State Department report, Syria is a destination country for women from Asia, Europe, and other Arab countries who are trafficked as domestic servants and prostitutes. Women and children from the Iraqi refugee community have been subjected to commercial sexual exploitation in Syria, and then exported to Kuwait, Lebanon, and the United Arab Emirates for forced prostitution.

POSSIBLE MEASURES

1. Control of the Border

Stopping the flow of arms and fighters into Iraq should be our immediate priority. A multipronged strategy would involve introducing U.N. Security Council resolutions calling upon Syria to tighten border security, increasing coalition forces on the Iraqi side of the border, freezing Syrian assets and accounts outside the country so as to disrupt the movement of funds, and requesting a boycott of Damascus International Airport until tighter controls are implemented. (Many major European carriers still serve Damascus.)

The Syrian town of Abu Kamal, only a few miles from the Iraqi border,

A U.S. soldier patrols the Syria-Iraq border

is a major planning and organizational center for insurgents. A small incursion of coalition forces would be sufficient to take control of the town—a move unlikely to be met with objection from the international community, particularly if U.N. demands for border security have not been acknowledged. Abu Kamal could then be used as a base for further operations within Syria.

2. Support of Opposition Groups

Four decades of repression and brutality have given rise to a wide spectrum of opposition to Bashar, both within the country and abroad. In

Bashar al-Assad

2005, the Beirut-Damascus Declaration was signed by various dissident parties, calling for comprehensive change in Syrian government. The U.S. should actively support these groups—particularly now, amid signs of an impending crackdown on signatories to the declaration. At present, there is no clear opposition leader who could provide these groups with focus and coordination; therefore, the United States must use its intelligence assets to identify and support a capable candidate, in effect picking a winner that would then be directed to galvanize resistance.

Outside Syria, opposition is similarly broad, with notable groups based in London, Paris, and Beirut. In September 2007, a General Secretariat was set up under the leadership of Mamoun al-Homsi to coordinate the activities of these various entities and speak with one voice from outside Syria. Homsi is a former prisoner of the Assad regime, and enjoys support from the exile community. The well-organized Syrian National Council should also be seen as a possible framework for a new administration.

3. Regime Change from Within

Dissent within Syria's ruling elite is on the rise; several senior officials have been purged from power, and Ghazi Kenaan, who was rumored to have been plotting a coup with a former vice president and military chief, was recently assassinated. Assad is dependent upon an ever-shrinking inner circle, and tensions have been reported between Bashar, his brother Maher, and his brother-in-law Asef Shawkat, both of whom wield considerable influence. While augmenting opposition groups, the United States should also explore opportunities to contact members of the ruling elite and exiled former officials sympathetic to U.S. aims and the desires of Syria's increasingly vocal population. In the event of a coup, the United States should be prepared to immediately and, if necessary, aggressively support a new administration.

4. Mobilization of the Kurds

The concentration of Syria's oppressed Kurdish population in the northeast of the country presents a strategic opportunity. In Iraq, the northern provinces under the control of the Kurdistan Regional Government (KRG) have achieved great stability and political independence since 2003, providing a model for other parts of the region. As a reliable U.S. ally, the KRG would doubtless support any efforts, diplomatic or otherwise, to liberate Syrian Kurds, and coalition forces could expect full cooperation from Kurdish fighters on both sides of the Iraq-Syria border. Such a strategy could have the dual effect of destabilizing the Assad regime and advancing U.S. efforts to bring peace to Iraq and the region.

The KRG could be promised sovereignty over a newly liberated Kurdish region of Syria in exchange for relinquishing its separatist claims in Kurdish Turkey. Such a compromise might persuade Turkey to join a U.S.-Kurdish coalition aimed at wresting Kurdish Syria from Damascus. Were Assad to lose control of so much Syrian territory, the support he depends on from senior military officials and conservative segments of the population would vanish, greatly facilitating efforts at regime change. If successful, this approach could be quickly applied in the Kurdish areas of northwest Iran.

5. Precision Strikes

A program of limited air strikes against Syrian military installations could be launched from coalition bases in Iraq and U.S. carriers in the Mediterranean. Syria's air force is inadequate and its air defenses poor; its navy is plagued by mismanagement and obsolete equipment. U.S. forces would be essentially unopposed.

A first round of strikes would be directed at known chemical and biological weapons manufacturing and storage sites, including concrete shelters in the Palmyra region, caves near Damascus, and an anthrax production facility near Homs, as well as any suspected stockpiles of nuclear materials. Anti-air defenses should be targeted next, followed by missile stockpiles, Hezbollah supply depots and training camps, foreign-fighter encampments near the Iraqi border, and oil fields at Suwaydiyah, Qaratshui, Rumayian, and Tayyem.

The recent strike by Israeli warplanes shows the ease with which such missions can be carried out; Israel could play a partnership role in any future operations.

6. Invasion

While a full-scale invasion is the least desirable path, the United States must prepare for the possibility that Syrian belligerence will make one unavoidable. An invasion plan would begin with an expanded program of air strikes, focusing on those targets detailed and also on artillery and tank batteries, missile production facilities near Aleppo and Hama, and test sites. Once Syrian response capability had been degraded, ground forces would be introduced through Lebanon and the Golan Heights, moving quickly to take Damascus, while coalition forces and Kurdish fighters stationed in Iraq would move across the borders to the south and east. Turkish cooperation from the north is also an option.

Syrian forces are poorly trained and badly equipped. Morale is low, and the military lacks experienced and effective officers and planners. Corruption is endemic. Many Syrian brigades could be expected to surrender or flee, and those that fought would be easily overcome. Faced with penetration at three borders and aerial devastation of its military facilities, Damascus is likely to fall more quickly than Baghdad.

The Syrian population, which has suffered under consecutive Assad dictatorships for thirty-eight years, will hardly object to the removal of the regime. Priority should be placed on keeping water, electricity, and waste and transportation services intact in population centers, and on working with local governments to keep order. Widespread sectarian violence is unlikely in overwhelmingly Sunni Syria, and Kurdish forces should be warned against expansionist activities. A quick defeat of Assad will allow withdrawal of U.S. forces within weeks or months, thus avoiding the post-invasion difficulties faced in Iraq.

The entrance of Hezbollah into ground combat is a possibility in this scenario. However, Israel Defense Forces (IDF) could be enlisted to minimize its involvement.

CONCLUSION

The occupation of Iraq has emboldened Syria. With Iran, it has become an active supporter of the insurgency, and hopes to control the region after a U.S. withdrawal. The sacrifice of U.S. blood and treasure in Iraq will be irrelevant if the result is a set of nuclear-armed terrorist-funding states dedicated to eliminating every Western interest within reach. Surrounded by a nuclear Iran and Syria, the new Iraq would be highly vulnerable, necessitating the permanent presence of large numbers of American troops. Even the status quo—a free flow of arms and fighters from Syria into Iraq, steady support of Hezbollah, development of weapons of mass destruction, defiance of the international community—is unacceptable.

The United States must begin exploring its options in Syria. The Assad regime is committed to standing in the way of peace and stability. Removing it is the only way to dispel the troubles of the region.

SUDAN

The Sudanese government's support of terrorist groups poses a direct threat to global security. And the genocidal crisis in Darfur and eastern Chad demands immediate humanitarian intervention.

ABSTRACT

• Sudan is controlled by an Islamicist regime with strong ties to terrorism. Its capital, Khartoum, has served as a worldwide center for militant Islamism and one-time home to Osama bin Laden.

• President Omar al-Bashir's regime is founded on Arab supremacism. He has hoarded power and wealth through acts of systematic violence against Sudan's non-Arab populations.

• For years, the Sudanese government has recruited and armed janjaweed militias and dispatched them to commit brutality against defenseless civilians. These horseback militias terrorize the refugee population, killing and raping indiscriminately, and block humanitarian aid, causing widespread death by starvation and malnutrition.

• In Sudan's Darfur region, more than two hundred thousand people have died as a result of these raids. Two and a half million Sudanese have been displaced to neighboring countries, with millions more internally displaced. The humanitarian catastrophe has taxed Sudan's nine neighboring countries, destabilizing the Horn of Africa.

• Sudan's fractured, insecure state has allowed terrorist cells to seep back into the country. Al Qaeda–linked groups now train insurgents in Sudan before sending them to Iraq.

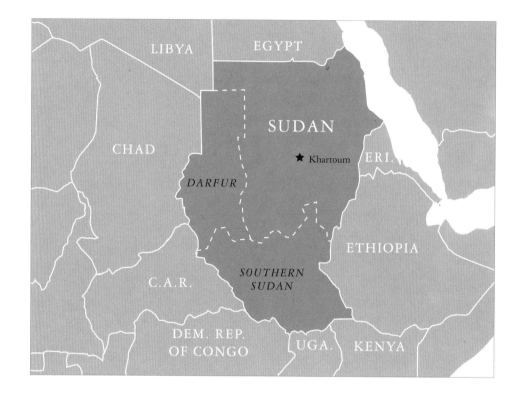

- The government of Sudan is dominated by a clique of radical Islamic
  fundamentalists who are unresponsive to international diplomacy. They
  will continue to wreak havoc on Sudan and the region until they are
  removed from power.

INTRODUCTION

After four years of genocide in Darfur, the United States has a moral,
ethical, and legal obligation to intervene and bring peace to the region.
The humanitarian disaster is spiraling out of control—the Sudanese government only rarely allows aid to reach vast refugee camps in Darfur and
eastern Chad, leaving hundreds of thousands with unpredictable access
to food and protection. As aid organizations withdraw, violence against
refugees and internally displaced people (IDPs) has begun to escalate
once again. In addition, the government's long-standing support of international terrorist groups and jihadist networks has recently increased.

Bloor Gladstone 416-393-7674

Toronto Public Library

User ID: 2 ********* 8816

Date Format: DD/MM/YYYY

Number of Items: 1

Item ID:37131173775610
 Title:Where to invade next
 Date due:28/04/2018

Telephone Renewal# 416-395-5505
www.torontopubliclibrary.ca
 Saturday, April 7, 2018   5:03 PM

Bloor/Gladstone
Toronto Public Library
Bloor/Gladstone
416-393-7674

Payment date: 07 April 2018
17:02

Bill reason: REFERRAL
Original bill: $5.00

REFERRAL: $2.50
Total Paid: $2.50

Telephone Renewal 416-395-5505
www.torontopubliclibrary.ca

Al Qaeda has resumed its presence in Sudan, and insurgents are being trained there for the fighting in Iraq.

Both crises have been prolonged by the small group of radical ideologues who have controlled the government for decades. Ensconced in Khartoum, they disseminate Arab supremacism and Islamic fundamentalism as national policy. Diplomatic measures—sanctions, African Union (AU) peacekeeping missions, U.N. resolutions, and regional peace talks—have been ineffective in stopping their crimes. The United States must act now.

THREAT OVERVIEW

1. Islamofascism

An extremist Sunni Islamist organization called the Muslim Brotherhood controls all levers of state power in Sudan. It is dedicated to the establishment of Islamic law (sharia) within its borders and the spread of militant jihad beyond them. Sudan's religious figurehead is a radical cleric named Hassan al-Turabi, well known for imposing a harsh form of sharia throughout Sudan and endorsing amputations and hangings as punishments for small offenses. Al-Turabi is a powerful leader in the world of Islamic militancy, and has called for the complete restructuring of modern society, one that installs radical Islam as civilization's new

President Omar al-Bashir

foundation. "I admit we are a threat to the present world order," he has said. "We seek to correct the world order."

2. Genocide

In 2003, two non-Arab African groups in Darfur, the Sudan Liberation Army (SLA) and the Justice and Equality Movement (JEM), challenged

Bashir's government after decades of neglect and oppression. The government's response was to employ thousands of local Arab nomads—

Janjaweed militiamen

mercenaries who shared its racist ideology—to take up arms and attack non-Arab villages. Musa Hilal of the Um Jalul tribe, the outlaw who currently leads these janjaweed miltias, confirmed the government's role during a rare videotaped interview with Human Rights Watch: "All of the people in the field are led by top army commanders… These people get their orders from the western command center, and from Khartoum."

Specific ethnic groups are being singled out for violence. Just as the

A Darfuri village attacked by janjaweed

Tutsis were targeted in Rwanda, three non-Arab black African tribes are being targeted in Darfur: the Zaghawa, the Massaleit, and the Fur. Abetted by direct support and intelligence from the Sudanese government, and with the cooperation of ground troops and air assaults by Sudan's military, these proxy militias are destroying entire communities in Darfur. Tens of thousands of unarmed civilians are being murdered, tortured, and raped.

The janjaweed militias act with total impunity; as payment, the Sudanese government allows them to seize as much land and livestock as they can. Humanitarian organizations monitoring the crisis have reported horrific atrocities: dismemberment, mass executions, women gang-raped, children thrown into fires. As part of the government's "scorched earth" campaign, entire crops have been burned to destroy food sources, and dead bodies have been thrown into wells to corrupt fresh-water supplies.

Khartoum's agenda of ethnic cleansing is now reaching a new stage: repopulation of the lands where Zaghawa, Fur, and Massaleit groups have been killed or expelled with new ethnically Arab settlers. The regime's ultimate aim is complete social and political reengineering. Unless it is stopped, the Sudanese government will never allow Darfur's displaced millions to return home. This would create catastrophic consequences throughout the region.

3. Refugees

At least two hundred thousand lives have been claimed in Darfur, but that may well be only the beginning. More than two and a half million Darfuri survivors fled their communities and now live in refugee camps in neighboring countries. Millions more reside in camps for IDPs within Sudan. Three and one-half million people in the region currently depend on humanitarian aid for basic survival. Yet these groups continue to be terrorized by janjaweed militia forces and the government's military. Janjaweed militias regularly encircle the camps, attacking and raping female refugees who venture out for firewood along the camps' perimeters. The Sudanese military, despite international sanctions, brutally attacks its

Refugees from Darfur

own people to this day: in 2007, military planes and helicopters were painted white—mimicking the color of U.N. humanitarian aircraft—in order to lure Darfuris toward them during bombing runs.

At the same time, President Bashir ruthlessly blocks humanitarian assistance from reaching Darfur. Humanitarian workers are frequently harassed and denied access to some of the worst-affected areas, where civilians are most vulnerable. When such pressure forced the World Food Programme to halve its rations for Darfur, 350,000 people were left without food. Aid organizations and relief workers are also routinely targeted for attacks. In July 2006, the U.N. and several other organizations began to pull out of Darfur due to the violence.

The fragile aid infrastructure is in danger of collapsing. If it does, deaths would reach a scale far worse than what has been seen thus far.

4. Human Rights

The human rights record of the Sudanese government and its autocratic leaders is abysmal. The age-old practice of slavery persists in Sudan—for many years, Arab northerners have enslaved black Africans from the south. As of 2007, some estimates place the number of non-Muslim blacks still in slavery as high as two hundred thousand.

Secret police, meanwhile, employ tactics of civilian terror: political detainees are apprehended by plainclothes security forces late at night and brought to unofficial security sites called "ghost houses" in Khartoum, El Obeid, Port Sudan, and more remote towns. Detainees are tried by secret military tribunals or simply not tried at all, and torture is routine. Escapees from ghost houses have reported being subjected to electrocution, severe beatings, rape, water torture, mock executions, and the pulling out of fingernails. Treatment often concludes with the victims being "disappeared" or extrajudicially executed.

The Khartoum regime prevents international investigators from visiting detainees, and human-rights monitors have been routinely denied access to detention facilities. The true extent of violations occurring in ghost houses will not be known until the Bashir regime is forced to furnish comprehensive lists and locations of detainees and comply with international law.

5. Regional Insecurity and Cross-Border Attacks

The Darfur crisis has affected every one of Sudan's nine neighboring states, and threatens to destroy the tenuous political balance in the Horn of Africa. Refugees from Darfur have spilled over into Chad, Ethiopia, Kenya, the Central African Republic, the Democratic Republic of the Congo, Egypt, and Uganda, all of which have been forced to provide shelter for the displaced. The influx of Sudanese refugees places unbearable burdens on these neighbors, exhausting their resources and increasing regional tensions.

But the refugees are not the only problem: the violence has also spread across Darfur's borders, especially into the lawless regions of eastern Chad. The Sudanese government is now supporting an insurgency against the Chadian government in N'Djamena by launching armed attacks from Darfur. Janjaweed militias are attacking Chadian civilians, and more than one hundred thousand Chadians have been displaced. Violence against Chadian women and children has become widespread. Cross-border attacks have enflamed ethnosectarian violence between Chadian groups as well—janjaweed militias have provided organizational support to Arab militias in Chad, who then target non-Arab Chadians from the Dajo and Muro tribes.

Chadian rebels cross the Sudanese border

Without forceful and immediate action, the entire Horn of Africa is likely to unhinge. The next Darfur could very well be in eastern Chad.

6. Support of al Qaeda

In the last decade, Sudan has positioned itself as a center for pan-Islamic militancy. In the 1990s it began holding annual meetings for terrorist leaders, hoping to unite anti-American militant groups from North Africa and the Middle East into a cohesive force for international jihad. Most notoriously, the Bashir regime has long-standing ties to al Qaeda.

Osama bin Laden built his network of terror in Sudan; the Bashir regime hosted him from 1991 through 1996. In 1998, al Qaeda members based in Sudan bombed the U.S. embassies in Kenya and Tanzania, killing 224 people. In 2000, the Sudanese government provided money, weapons, explosives, logistical support, diplomatic passports, and other materials to an al Qaeda operation in Yemen that culminated in the bombing of the USS *Cole*, which killed seventeen U.S. military personnel.

In 2001, a Sudanese man was arrested for planning to bomb the U.S. embassy in New Delhi with explosives provided by the Sudanese government. And in May 2003, al Qaeda reopened a camp in western Sudan and began training Islamist operatives recruited from the Arab world. The Bashir regime allowed them to operate in spite of the government's "official" post-9/11 policy of noncompliance with terrorists.

The Sudanese government has also enlisted the support of Islamist groups in the Darfur genocide. Since the eruption of the conflict there, Osama bin Laden and other al Qaeda leaders have made repeated calls for jihadists to join the fight. In late 2006, three al Qaeda training camps were discovered in the north Darfur region of El Fasher–Kabkabiya, preparing Arab militants to fight alongside the janjaweed militias.

The training camps in Sudan also serve as staging grounds for fighters en route to the Iraqi insurgency. Countless Sudanese and foreign nationals who transited through Sudan have been captured fighting in Iraq.

POSSIBLE MEASURES

1. Diplomacy and Sanctions

All measures of international diplomacy have been exhausted with the Bashir regime. Immediate, comprehensive, and targeted multilateral sanctions on Khartoum and the senior government officials responsible for orchestrating the Darfur genocide should be put in place. These should include a strictly enforced arms embargo and a targeted blockade of Port Sudan to stop shipments of arms from China and Russia. Border security should be heightened to prevent arms flow, cross-border attacks, and the free migration of insurgents into Iraq. While ideally this effort would be spearheaded by the U.N. Security Council, China and Russia would likely veto comprehensive measures. U.S. leadership will be required.

2. Humanitarian Intervention

The seven-thousand-strong African Union peacekeeping force, deployed in 2005, was severely ill-equipped, undertrained, and lacking in both funding and motivation. It suffered constant sabotage by janjaweed militias and manipulation by the Sudanese government. Recently a larger force of twenty-six thousand was proposed, but this mission will likely also be insufficient. In the meantime, civilians in Darfur will starve.

Rather than wait for the U.N., the United States should quickly act to effect peace in Sudan. Where previous peacekeeping missions have failed, a strong U.S.-led humanitarian force would succeed. Our objective would not differ from that of previous plans; in fact, the joint U.N./African Union UNAMID resolution offers an instructive blueprint for humanitarian intervention in Darfur, and its broad support in the U.N. Security Council offers an incentive for its adoption—the United States could intervene on the grounds that it is enforcing an existing resolution.

It is widely accepted that if similar action had been taken in Rwanda, the genocide of 1994 could have been avoided. The international community is undivided in its support for ending the violence in Darfur, and U.S. military intervention would attract a broad multilateral coalition. Britain and France have already suggested action in Darfur, and NATO member countries could be counted on to supply peacekeeping troops.

Regional support from Africa would come easily. Logistically, Chad would be essential—French air bases there are well-situated for air operations, and the United States has substantial military assets in Chad's capital, Djibouti. French and Chadian troops are already stationed along the eastern border with Darfur. Chadian president Idriss Déby supports the UNAMID intervention, and Chad would likely join a U.S.-led humanitarian legion.

Current U.S. military presence elsewhere throughout Africa is considerable: bases are located in Uganda and Dakar, and smaller outposts exist in Algeria and Mauritania. U.S. military envoys could escort logistical supply convoys to ensure the safe provision of aid during any operation, and ground troops could protect aid workers from attacks. Humanitarian access corridors would be reopened and secured, allowing safe return for refugees along secured migration routes.

3. No-Fly Zone and Buffer Zones

U.S. peacekeeping troops should also enforce and monitor a cease-fire while securing refugee camps and protecting the civilians of Darfur. A no-fly zone could be established over affected areas in western Sudan, where Sudanese warplanes are still bombing villages as a prelude to janjaweed militia attacks. The no-fly zone would end the aerial attacks and disrupt support for the janjaweed militias. The imposition of the zone would be fairly easy, requiring only a dozen or two dozen fighter aircraft out of Chad, flanked by NATO air support.

Conventional troops would create demilitarized safe havens on the ground in Darfur, establishing buffer zones around camps. These forces would patrol the buffer zones and establish checkpoints to protect refugees and defend against attacks. Community police forces would recruit female officers to receive reports of crimes against women and help combat widespread sexual violence.

4. Air Strikes on Terrorist Groups

Part and parcel of humanitarian intervention is the rooting out of al Qaeda terrorist cells in Sudan. Any intervention must include strategic air strikes on terrorist training centers, followed by ground forces inserted to capture terrorist leaders. This would destabilize the janjaweed militias' connections to powerful insurgent groups and generally ease the flow of U.S. humanitarian intervention. Swift surprise attacks carried out by American special forces on the camps near El Fasher–Kabkabiya would be necessary to fully demobilize al Qaeda's presence in the region.

5. Action Against the Regime

Stability in Sudan can be achieved at reasonable cost. The official Sudanese military is small and unsophisticated, and has depended for many years on proxy militia forces. While these horseback militias are capable of annihilating unarmed civilian populations, they are disorganized and weak; disarming and demobilizing them would be a central and simple tenet of the peace operation. U.S.-led forces could locate and neutralize all armed forces in Sudan, both regular and irregular, within the first few weeks of intervention. Supply routes would be cut and heavy weaponry confiscated.

Airpower would be a deciding factor in Sudan. Preemptive bombing campaigns on key airstrips, hangars, and command-and-control centers would quickly dismantle Sudan's military power. NATO could supply considerable assistance, and it is likely that the U.S. Air Force would only need to contribute a few hundred precision-weapon aircraft and about a dozen air tankers for refueling. American bases situated in the Middle East, especially in Saudi Arabia, as well as aircraft carriers in the Red Sea, would facilitate operations.

Troop contributions would also be minimal. After the genocide in Rwanda, it was determined that about fifteen hundred troops could have prevented the deaths of eight hundred thousand people. The U.S.-led operation in Sudan, bolstered by African Union and U.N. peacekeepers, would include military units from NATO members and concerned nations around the globe. In Britain, five thousand troops have been put on standby for deployment to Darfur, and more than fifty other countries have already contributed peacekeepers. The United States would, at most, need to supply ten thousand troops.

CONCLUSION

After years of Khartoum's noncompliance and the failure of humanitarian missions, the only effective response to the situation in Sudan is military intervention. The international community has traditionally responded to genocides with the promise of "never again." This is now being said about Darfur, even as violence continues and hundreds of thousands of additional lives are put at risk. Millions of civilians need protection, major relief operations need security, and Darfuris need to return to their homes if the region is to maintain any sort of stability. The refugee crisis now threatens to devolve into war between Chad and Sudan and complete chaos in the Horn of Africa, chaos that would function as a welcome mat for America's enemies. The Sudanese government will continue to drag events down this road until Bashir's genocidal regime is removed from power.

.

NORTH KOREA

North Korea is a desperate, damaged nation with confirmed links to the nuclear black market. Its leader, Kim Jong-il, is a delusional, ruthless dictator bent on East Asian supremacy. With the help of his secret police and a corrupt army driven more by self-enrichment than ideology, Kim holds absolute control over a starving, repressed populace that is completely cut off from the outside world. Under his rule, North Korea has a single purpose: to increase its power by any means necessary, including the sale of nuclear technology, the mass murder of its own people, and sophisticated state-sponsored terror.

ABSTRACT

- North Korea commands the fourth-largest army in the world. It also possesses an active nuclear program that has already passed the weapons-testing phase.

- Destitute and short of food, the North Korean people are subjugated by totalitarian repression, concentration camps, and complete international quarantine.

- The corrupt elite, the secret police, and the military leadership sustain themselves only by profits from drug trafficking, arms dealing, counterfeiting, and other criminal activities.

- The Kim regime has shown itself to be immune to diplomatic channels, and Kim has long manipulated the United States and its allies. He is interested only in cementing his own position.

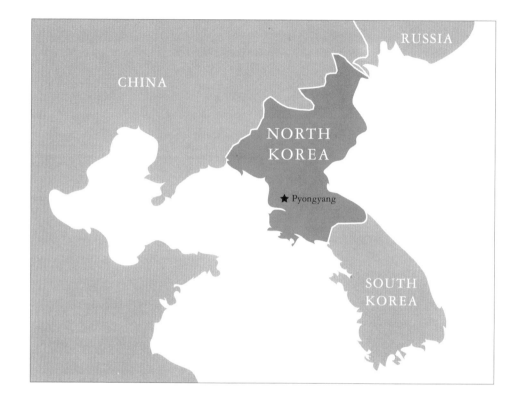

- Kim Jong-il is willing to do anything to protect his power, including providing nuclear technology to terrorists, murdering his people, and launching nuclear attacks on South Korean, Japanese, and U.S. soil.

- The clean assassination of Kim, followed by economic negotiations designed to remove the nation's nuclear program, will neutralize the North Korean threat, creating a contained state that holds new promise for its people.

INTRODUCTION

The Democratic People's Republic of Korea (DPRK) was established in 1948, three years after the U.N.—facing a conflict between Russia and the United States over joint trusteeship—divided Korea at the thirty-eighth parallel in the wake of Japanese occupation. The nation takes up the northern portion of the Korean peninsula, sharing borders with

China and Russia to the north and South Korea along the demilitarized zone (DMZ).

The dissolution of the USSR removed North Korea's main food supply, economic base, and ideological ally. Isolated and self-reliant, with few trading partners and arable land that amounts to only 18 percent of its territory, the country plunged toward bankruptcy in the 1990s. Flood, drought, and famine killed an estimated two million North Korean citizens between 1990 and 1997. In the midst of this crisis, "Dear Leader" Kim Jong-il came to power. Rather than facing his country's problems, his "Military First" policy created two distinct North Koreas: a corrupt and privileged militarized elite; and a starving majority kept in line through labor camps, imprisonment, execution, and ideological terror. The nation's resources, meanwhile, were channeled to chilling aims. In October 2006, North Korea tested its first nuclear device, confirming the progress of its atomic weapons program. Long-range missile delivery systems were tested in 2007.

Korean officials guard the demilitarized zone

THREAT OVERVIEW

1. The Nuclear State and the Failure of Diplomacy

North Korea has impoverished itself and alienated its neighbors in order to acquire, build, and sustain its nuclear program. Western intelligence sources agree that the secret program to develop highly enriched uranium (HEU) had begun by 1997, three years into Kim's rule. It continued unchecked through years of deceitful, time-buying diplomatic posturing, and barely slowed in 2002, when the United States confronted North Korea with evidence of its active nuclear program and defiance of many pledges and treaties—a program that North Korea readily confirmed. The United States failed to act decisively at that juncture, engaging instead in ineffective negotiation tactics. More years were lost.

Today, at least two programs appear to be firmly in place. One, focused on plutonium, is advanced enough to produce six to twelve nuclear weapons. The other is based on uranium-enrichment equipment believed to have been obtained from Abdul Qadeer Khan, the father of the Pakistani bomb.

The last decade has been marked by a complex dance of diplomatic maneuvering that has yielded North Korea appeasement and bailout aid. Neither Secretary of State Madeleine Albright's meetings in Pyongyang, nor South Korea's "Sunshine Policy," nor Japanese prime minister Junichiro Koizumi's joint declaration with Kim, nor China's reduction of subsidies, nor the series of three- and six-party talks since 2003, nor U.N. sanctions have shown any signs of stopping North Korea's nuclear program. Again and again allowed the benefit of the doubt, North Korea has broken virtually every promise it has ever made to the international community. At every turn, it has moved closer to nuclear aggression.

2. A Desperate People

With millions dead already from hunger, malnutrition remains an epidemic in North Korea. NGOs estimate that as many as three hundred thousand citizens have risked their lives to escape the country, which is kept tightly closed to the outside world. Repression of information, free speech, and opposition is absolute. Over the last thirty years, massacres of civilians have occurred in Chongjin, Hamhung, Musan, Onsong, and Songrim.

Concentration camps and prison labor centers are used by Kim's regime to contain any sign of dissent. Mortality-rate estimates for these camps range from 4 to 20 percent, with former captives reporting beatings, starvation, executions, and forced termination of pregnancies.

Despite these measures, North Korean citizens continue to risk their lives in acts of civil opposition. In November 2006, a mass protest in Hoeryong was reported after authorities tried to shut down a legal market—it was perhaps the largest protest since the 1998 labor demonstrations in Songrim, which were ended by tank assault. The increasingly desperate and disobedient populace represents a destabilizing pressure on Kim and a potential wedge for any outside actor.

3. Endemic Corruption in Military

In early 2007, a Japanese NGO documented simple procedures for bribing North Korean border guards and smuggling humanitarian supplies into North Hamgyong Province. A growing stream of refugees into South Korea and China also attests to the increasing ease with which people are able to buy their way out of North Korea. This wave of border bribery has led to a spike in video and information smuggling, with an increasing number of documentaries and news reports landing in the West.

More systemic, however, has been the rise of corrupt officials taking personal profit from state-sanctioned drug trafficking, arms deals, and extortion. Piracy by the North Korean navy has been ongoing since the 1990s, and U.S. embassy reports of a 1995 army revolt in North Hamgyong appear to paint a picture of elite factions warring over opium profits. Extra-national smuggling partners report increased high-level cooperation in their activities, even as government executions for smuggling are on the rise. The use of diplomatic pouches for the transport and sale of narcotics and other contraband has been confirmed.

Combined, these illicit activities suggest a restive, selfish government class, less interested in principled resistance than in its own indulgence. At the same time, the underpinnings of this corrupt economy have been impaired. After six years of growth despite increasing isolation, the North Korean economy contracted by 1.1 percent in 2006, according to South Korean reports. Research reported in *Newsweek* pointed to sanctions aimed at North Korea's contraband economy: the shutting-down of a Macao-based bank central to money-laundering activities; actions to reduce missile sales to customers in Syria, Iran, Pakistan, and elsewhere; a crackdown on several counterfeiting operations; a curtailment of the market in endangered species; and general interference aimed at smugglers. Revenue from arms sales and contraband may have accounted for as much as half of North Korea's income from exports before actions in recent years reduced this percentage by two-thirds. The elite is, for once, feeling the pinch, and may welcome changed circumstances.

4. An All-Powerful Dictator with Links to Terror

Although known to his people as "Dear Leader," Kim Jong-il's official title is the Chairman of the National Defense Commission, Supreme

Juche tower in Pyongyang

Commander of the Korean People's Army, and General Secretary of the Workers' Party of Korea. Although his official biography places his birth at a secret camp atop Korea's highest mountain, occasioned by "a double rainbow and a new star in the sky," he was born in Vyatskoye, a fishing village in eastern Russia where his father and predecessor, Kim Il Sung, lived in exile.

Kim is driven by ideology, his legacy as a "living god," and a variety of nationalism that includes a policy of self-reliance known as *juche.*

He has been implicated in the 1983 Rangoon bombing that killed seventeen officials from South Korea, including four cabinet members, as well as in the 1987 Korean Air bombing. Confirmed reports of North Korean abductions of Japanese citizens in the late '70s and '80s ordered by Kim's father have been echoed by accounts of more recent abductions, including those of two South Korean celebrities captured to jump-start North Korea's film industry and of young women kidnapped to serve as Kim's personal companions.

Kim has survived five known coup attempts; he had ten officers burned at the stake in 1994 for conspiring to assassinate him. It has been reported that he uses as least two body doubles for public appearances. To protect himself, his power, and what he sees as his family's place in history, Kim has made it clear that he is prepared to use nuclear weapons—through escalation, threats, sale, terror acts, or even direct strikes.

5. The Atomic Fire Sale

In 2007, Israel conducted air strikes in Syria targeted at sites containing elements of a nascent nuclear program provided by North Korea. An anonymous former senior Bush administration official—who at one time had full access to intelligence on both countries—issued the "very sobering assessment that North Korea is the world's No. 1 proliferator and a country willing to sell whatever it possesses."

A North Korean nuclear facility in Yongbyon

North Korea is a known trafficker in narcotics, missiles, information, and kidnapping victims, but its worst offense may be its willingness to bring its nuclear program into the black market. This is how North Korea itself originally obtained its technology and expertise, and both Kim Jong-il and the corrupt elite are now being driven to find such new sources of revenue. North Korea is poised to sell its nuclear technology to the highest bidder, at its earliest opportunity.

6. The Price of Inaction

For half a century, hopeful bureaucrats and politicians have waited for the situation in North Korea to resolve itself. Now we are faced with the costs—an intransigent, unstable state, and no good option for a ground invasion. Though we would win an all-out war, unacceptable losses would be sustained by South Korean and U.S. forces. Seoul lies in easy range of North Korea's artillery—hundreds of 170mm KOKSAN guns and multiple-launch rocket systems fitted with artillery shells and chemical weapons. In a full-scale military confrontation, the South Korean capital would be destroyed within hours. In addition, North Korea has as many as six hundred Scud missiles; with its No-Dong missiles, it could hit Japan. Ground units could fire up to five hundred thousand artillery rounds per hour against South Korean defenses, and at the thirty-seven thousand American troops based in the demilitarized zone. One U.S. military estimate posits—without taking into account the very real possibility of a deliverable nuclear weapon—that U.S. and South Korean forces could suffer up to five hundred thousand casualties within the first ninety days of military action, along with hundreds of thousands of civilian casualties.

POSSIBLE MEASURES

1. Assassinate Kim Jong-il

Kim Jong-il represents the center of nuclear proliferation among America's enemies. Even today, with his nation disintegrating before his eyes,

Kim Jong-il

Kim has no intention of abandoning his nuclear ambitions. As income from narcotics, conventional weapons, and other smuggling dwindles, the astronomical sums available for nuclear sales to terrorists are, increasingly, his best and most realistic opportunity to save his regime.

If Kim resists this option, corrupt bosses within the army and the elite—the "Sopranos" of North Korea, as described by *U.S. News and World Report*—may take matters into their own hands. They have no real allegiance to the state, and have already transitioned from terror to extortion to narcotics in pursuit of economic gain; they are well-positioned and well-connected to smuggle nuclear materials, technologies, and plans.

Threatened by their dissolving loyalties and his own loss of control over his atomic trump card, history suggests that Kim will act aggressively. He would not hesitate to enshrine himself and his nation in martyrdom rather than lose power or face defeat. Under his continued leadership, nuclear strikes by North Korea are a real possibility, the sale of nuclear technology is all but certain, and the end of the age of nuclear deterrence is in sight.

Kim must be killed. The United States should dispatch assassins whose providence appears to be internal, or who at least possess a formal patina of plausible denial. If they fail once, they will likely have another opportunity—previous attempts, originating in the army and North Korean underground movements, have been carefully downplayed by the regime and dealt with out of public sight.

2. Overtures to the North Korean "Sopranos"

After Kim's assassination, the United States, along with China, Russia, Japan, and South Korea, should open negotiations with North Korea's corrupt elite, recognizing its leadership over any succession by Kim's sons or toadies. These talks will be positioned as a clean-slate opportunity to examine all North Korean positions, including disarmament, sanctions, international status, and aid packages.

Secretly, we would already be negotiating through indirect smuggling channels. Prior to Kim's destruction, income flows would be opened to these corrupt underbosses, identifying the most self-motivated and enterprising candidates for cooperation. Our most promising partners will be regional bosses with both the autonomy for ambition and close ties to Kim's inner circle.

In the wake of Kim's death, there may arise a radical "Dear Leader" cult bent on escalating confrontation, but cracks within the army have shown a growing weariness of Kim, and the majority of North Korean leadership is motivated by power and profit, not ideology or martyrdom. Overtures must make clear the enormous opportunities available to captains of the new North Korean ship.

3. Increase Internal and External Pressure on Post-Kim Regime

By covertly assisting underground groups within the country and tightening sanction measures that have strangled North Korea's illicit economy, the United States could work to make sure any new regime faces increasing soft threats to its future. Evidence points to growing desire for change within the populace; the demise of Kim would no doubt require North Korea's military and army to violently repress its people and tighten its borders to maintain control.

In this scenario, both China and South Korea would move to secure their borders, but North Korean sovereignty must be respected at all costs. At that point, while the new regime found itself facing a situation in some ways more difficult than the one faced now by Kim, it would be granted expanded options to improve its economic situation, control its people, and remove the potential threats of blockade and further military action.

4. Implement a Graft for Nukes Program

Working with a regional six-nation group, with China as a lead player, the United States could offer a massive package of aid, trade agreements, and investment projects to the new leadership as the only way out of its economic and diplomatic quagmire—with the condition that North Korea "sell" its entire nuclear program to the group.

On the surface, such a package would allow the new regime to address its crippling economic problems, its food shortage, and its future, and provide continued funding for the massive military apparatus while also leaving the power of the elite intact. Privately, the United States would supplement these payments with enormous cash incentives to individual bosses. A six-nation agreement would also leave North Korea sovereign, with China and the United States safeguarding it from interference. Post-Kim, China will not want to confront the threat of the mass migration of refugees across its border; their interests too lie in an independent North Korea that can support its own population.

In many ways, the crooked bosses are the perfect leaders in the transition from today's isolated North Korea to a communist nation more fully engaged in the world economy. They understand the global state of affairs and recognize the position North Korea occupies in world politics. They recognize the potential in removing the single common threat that unites the United States and China and will imagine a chance to play us against one another for lasting security and immense profit. With the threat of blockade hanging overhead, these bosses would no doubt capitalize on the opportunity to cash in on a nuclear score more profitable than they had ever thought possible.

5. *Prepare a Contingency Preemptive Strike*

The United States has, of course, already prepared for the nightmare scenario. Should North Korea show intent to launch a nuclear attack after an unsuccessful assassination attempt or a bad turn by a new regime, we would strike preemptively at all weapons facilities and known launch sites.

Air and missile strikes stand a good chance of wiping out North Korea's nuclear program and weapons-delivery systems, but the extent of collateral damage is hard to estimate. Radioactive material from destroyed nuclear facilities could spread widely in North and South Korea, as well as in Japan and China, bringing with it extensive contamination and many civilian casualties. Seoul would in all likelihood be destroyed. If mobilized in time, intermediate No-Dong missiles could strike Japan and American bases, and long-range Taepo Dong missiles or their counterparts could strike the U.S. mainland.

CONCLUSION

Already the world's most volatile nuclear state, North Korea is poised to become the main force for global nuclear proliferation. Our policies of good-faith negotiations, diplomatic pressure, sanctions, and incentives have had no impact on its nuclear progress and intentions, and done nothing to lessen the ongoing humanitarian disaster.

Under Kim's narcissistic leadership, North Korea will soon sell nuclear weapons to America's state and non-state enemies. Kim Jong-il is the most dangerous man living today, erratic and without remorse. The safety of the United States and its friends across the globe requires that his life be taken.

SOURCES

UZBEKISTAN

"Deaths in Custody in Uzbekistan: Human Rights Watch Briefing Paper." *Human Rights Watch*. hrw.org/backgrounder/eca/uzbek040403-bck.htm.

"In the Chiller: Uzbekistan." *The Economist (US)* 380, no. 8486 (2006): 44US.

"Profile: Islam Karimov." http://news.bbc.co.uk/2/hi/asia-pacific/4554997.stm.

"Radicalism in Central Asia." Muslim Uzbekistan. http://muslimuzbekistan.net/en/centralasia/comments/story.php?ID=8576.

"Uzbekistan: Torture Death in Prison." *Human Rights Watch* (2003).

Allison, Roy, Lena Jonson, Utrikespolitiska Institutet (Sweden), and Royal Institute of International Affairs. Central Asian Security: The New International Context. London, Washington, D.C.: Royal Institute of International Affairs; Brookings Institution Press, 2001.

Becker, Gary S. "A Tale of Two Nations." *The Hoover Digest* Vol. 4 (1999).

Bureau of Democracy, Human Rights, and Labor. "Country Reports on Human Rights Practices: Uzbekistan." 2007.

Cohen, Ariel. "Uzbekistan's Eviction Notice: What Next." *Executive Memorandum*. www.heritage.org/Research/RussiaandEurasia/em978.cfm.

Heslin, Sheila. "Assessing Central Asia's Role in the Antiterror Campaign." *Policy Watch/Peace Watch*. www.washingtoninstitute.org/templateC05.php?CID=1440.

Hill, F., and K. Jones. "Fear of Democracy or Revolution: The Reaction to Andijon." *The Washington Quarterly* 29, no. 3 (2006): 111-25.

International Crisis Group. "Uzbekistan: Stagnation and Uncertainty." *Asia Briefing*. www.crisisgroup.org/library/documents/asia/central_asia/b67_uzbekistan___stagnation_and_uncertainty.pdf.

Kristol, William. "Springtime for Dictators? (Controlling of Dictators Is a Must to Control Terrorism)." *The Weekly Standard* 10, no. 39 (2005): 7(1).

Levitt, Matthew. "Next Steps in the War on Terrorism." *Policy Watch/Peace Watch*. www.washingtoninstitute.org/templateC05.php?CID=1488.

Luong, Pauline Jones, and Erika Weinthal. "New Friends, New Fears in Central Asia." *Foreign Affairs* 81, no. 2 (2002): 61.

McFaul, Michael. "The False Promise of Autocratic Stability." *The Weekly Standard* 11, no. 2 (2005): 45(1).

Paz, Reuven. "The Global Jihad Brotherhood: Egyptian Islamic Jihad and the Islamic Movement of Uzbekistan." *Policy Watch/Peace Watch*. www.washingtoninstitute.org/templateC05.php?CID=1439.

Saradzhyan, Simon. "Uzbekistan Seeks Russian Arms for Border Clashes." *Defense News* 15, no. 37 (2000): 8.

Schwartz, Stephen. "Andijan, Uzbekistan: One Year After; The Lessons We Should Learn from the Massacre." *The Weekly Standard* (2006): NA.

Schwartz, Stephen, and William Kristol. "Our Uzbek Problem." *The Weekly Standard* 10, no. 35 (2005): 9(1).

Stein, Lisa. "Of Protesters and Dictators." *U.S. News & World Report* 138, no. 20 (2005): 16.

Wright, R., and A.S. Tyson. "US Evicted from Air Base in Uzbekistan." *Washington Post* (2005): 1.

PHOTOS: Xinhua News Agency, U.S. Air Force, Associated Press, Ferghana.Ru Information Agency, Reuters

IRAN

Globalsecurity.org. www.globalsecurity.org/index.html.

"Iran's Islamic Militants Threaten to Strike U.S. Interests," *Agence France-Presse,* Dec. 28, 1996, p.1.

"Unacceptable. (Iran)." *National Review* 58, no. 8 (2006): 14.

Allison, Roy, Lena Jonson, Utrikespolitiska Institutet (Sweden), and Royal Institute of International Affairs. *Central Asian Security: The New International Context.* London, Washington, D.C.: Royal Institute of International Affairs; Brookings Institution Press, 2001.

Arkin, William M. "Early Warning." *The Washington Post.* http://blog.washingtonpost.com/earlywarning.

Bowen, Wyn Q., and Joanna Kidd. "The Iranian Nuclear Challenge." *International Affairs* 80, no. 2 (2004): 257-76.

Bruck, C. "Exiles: How Iran's Expatriates Are Gaming the Nuclear Threat." *New Yorker* (2006): 60.

Doron, Daniel. "Yes, Iran Can Be Stopped; The Iranian Regime Can't Live without Its Oil Money." *The Weekly Standard* (2007): NA.

Dowd, Maureen. "Axis of Sketchy Allies." *The New York Times* (2006): A11(L).

Friedman, Thomas L. "The First Law of Petropolitics: Iran's President Denies the Holocaust, Hugo Chavez Tells Western Leaders to Go to Hell, and Vladimir Putin Is Cracking the Whip. Why? They Know That the Price of Oil and the Pace of Freedom Always Move in Opposite Directions. It's the First Law of Petropolitics, and It May Be the Axiom to Explain Our Age." *Foreign Policy,* no. 154 (2006): 28(9).

Gerecht, Reuel Marc. "The Myth of Moderate Mullahs; It's Still Khomeini's Iran." *The Weekly Standard* 12, no. 26 (2007): NA.

———. "To Bomb, or Not to Bomb; That Is the Iran Question." *The Weekly Standard* 11, no. 30 (2006): NA.

Guitta, Olivier. "Sanctions against Iran Would Work; Too Bad They Won't Be Tried." *The Weekly Standard* (2007): NA.

Herman, Arthur. "Getting Serious About Iran: A Military Option." *Commentary* 122, no. 4 (2006): 28(5).

Hersh, S. "Last Stand: The Military's Problem with the President's Iran Policy." *New Yorker* 82, no. 21 (2006): 42.

Hersh, S. M. "The Iran Plans." *New Yorker* (2006): 30.

Kagan, Kimberly. "The Iran Dossier; Iraq Report VI: Iran's Proxy War Against the U.S. in Iraq." *The Weekly Standard* (2007): NA.

Lawson, Fred H. "Syria's Relations with Iran: Managing the Dilemmas of Alliance." *The Middle East Journal* 61, no. 1 (2007): 29(19).

Ledeen, Michael. "The Surge and Its Critics." *NationalReviewOnline.com.* http://article.nationalreview.com/q=ZTYxZDcxMzkzNzhiMzFkNTAwMzkxNjE0Y2FkNmM0MTE=.

Steorts, Jason Lee. "Can Iran Be Deterred? A Question We Cannot Afford to Get Wrong." *National Review* 58, no. 19 (2006): 30(4).

Loyola, Mario. "Before They Go Nuclear… Iran and the Question of Preemption." *National Review* 58, no. 15 (2006): 20(3).

Maloney, Suzanne. "Fear and Loathing in Tehran." *The National Interest,* no. 91 (2007): 42(7).

McInerney, Thomas. "Target: Iran; Yes, There Is a Feasible Military Option against the Mullahs' Nuclear Program." *The Weekly Standard* 11, no. 30 (2006): NA.

Milhollin, Gary. "Can Terrorists Get the Bomb?" *Commentary* 113, no. 2 (2002): 45(5).

Podhoretz, Norman. "The Case for Bombing Iran." *Commentary* 123, no. 6 (2007): 17(7).

Pollack, Kenneth M. *The Persian Puzzle: The Conflict between Iran and America.* 1st ed. New York: Random House, 2004.

Rubin, Michael. "Dangerous Cycle: North Korea, Iran, and Repetitive Diplomatic Failure." *American Enterprise Institute.* www.aei.org/publications/pubID.24626,filter.all/pub_detail.asp.

Sokolski, Henry. "Disarming the Mullahs: There Are Things We Can Do that Would Limit Their Options." *The Weekly Standard* 12, no. 6 (2006): NA.

Steorts, Jason Lee. "Axis Uber Alles? Bush Is Not Dealing Adequately with Iran and North Korea." *National Review* 59, no. 8 (2007): 26.

Taheri, Amir. "Getting Serious About Iran: For Regime Change." *Commentary* 122, no. 4 (2006): 21(7).

Williams, Walter E. "Will the West Defend Itself?" *Capitalism Magazine.* www.capmag.com/article.asp?ID=4768.

Wimbush, S. Enders. "The End of Deterrence; A Nuclear Iran Will Change Everything." *The Weekly Standard* (2007): NA.

Wurmser, Meyrav. "Up to No Good; Iran and Syria's Sinister Mideast Offensive Strikes Gaza and Lebanon." *The Weekly Standard* (2007): NA.

PHOTOS: Mehr News Agency, Hamed Saber, Government of Iran

PAKISTAN

"Afghan, Coalition Forces Destroy Taliban Heroin Lab." *American Forces Press Service.* www.defenselink.mil/news/newsarticle.aspx?id=47196.

"Al-Qaeda Is Thriving In Pakistan, Thanks to an Ill-Advised Ceasefire Deal That Pervez Musharraf Cut with Tribal Leaders in 2006." *National Review* 59, no. 14 (2007): 10.

"Barack Obama Rattled His Saber at Pakistan Early This Month." *National Review* 59, no. 15 (2007): 4.

"Could Pakistan Fall to Extremists?" *The Christian Science Monitor* (2007): 7.

"The Future of Kashmir." *BBC Online.* http://news.bbc.co.uk/2/shared/spl/hi/south_asia/03/kashmir_future/html/4.stm.

"Musharraf's Endgame: Pakistan." *The Economist (US)* 384, no. 8547 (2007): 54US.

"Who Is Hunting Whom? Afghanistan and Pakistan." *The Economist (US)* 384, no. 8542 (2007): 12US.

Armitage, Richard L., and Kara L. Bue. "Keep Pakistan on Our Side." *The New York Times* (2006); WK11(L).

Atal, Subodh. "Extremist, Nuclear Pakistan: An Emerging Threat?" *Cato Institute.* http://www.cato.org/pub_display.php?pub_id=1331.

Baker, Aryn. "Pakistan's Drama Unfolds." *Time International (Asia Edition)* 170, no. 12 (2007): 22.

Bose, Sumantra. *Kashmir: Roots of Conflict, Paths to Peace.* Cambridge, Mass.: Harvard University Press, 2003.

Darling, Dan. "Where the Taliban Still Rule; Not in Afghanistan, but in Pakistan." *The Weekly Standard* (2006): NA.

Dowd, Maureen. "Axis of Sketchy Allies." *The New York Times* (2006); A11(L).

Evans, Alexander. "Understanding Madrasahs." *Foreign Affairs* 85, no. 1 (2006): 9.

Fair, C. Christine. "Militant Recruitment in Pakistan: Implications for al Qaeda and Other Organizations." *Studies in Conflict and Terrorism* 27, no. 6 (2004): 489–504.

Gall, Carlotta. "At Border, Signs of Pakistani Role in Taliban Surge." *The New York Times* (2007): A1(L).

———. "Islamic Militants in Pakistan Bomb Targets Close to Home." *The New York Times* (2007): A1(L).

Gartenstein-Ross, Daveed, and Bill Roggio. "Pakistan Surrenders; The Taliban Control the Border with Afghanistan." *The Weekly Standard* 12, no. 3 (2006): NA.

Joscelyn, Thomas. "The Pakistan Connection; Pakistani Terror Networks Were Behind the 7/7

Bombings and the London Airline Plot. What Will We Do About It?" *The Weekly Standard* (2006): NA.

Koch, Andrew, and Jennifer Topping. "Pakistan's Nuclear-Related Facilities." Monitoring Proliferation Threats Project.

Latif, Aamir. "The Land of an Eye for an Eye; The Dangers of Going after the Taliban and Al Qaeda in Pakistan." *U.S. News & World Report* 143, no. 6 (2007): 36.

———. "Taliban and Al Qaeda Find 'Safe Haven' in Pakistan's No Man's Land." *U.S. News & World Report* (2007): NA.

Markey, Daniel. "A False Choice in Pakistan." *Foreign Affairs* 86, no. 4 (2007): 85.

Musharraf, Pervez. *In the Line of Fire: A Memoir*. New York: Free Press, 2006.

Nashat, Guity. "Some Sobering Thoughts on Pakistan's Future—and Ours." *National Review* 56, no. 7 (2004): 9.

Nickerson, Heather. "Action Update: May 24–June 6, 2004." *Center for Defense Information*. www.cdi. org/program/document.cfm?documentid=2250&programID=39&from_page=../friendlyversion/printversion.cfm

Omaar, Rageh. "We Must Get It Right In Pakistan." *New Statesman (1996)* 136, no. 4858 (2007): 20(1).

Peer, Basharat. "Papa-2." *n+1* (2007).

Raman, B. "Pakistan's Inter-Services Intelligence (ISI)." *South Asia Analysis Group*. www.saag.org/papers3/paper287.html.

Strmecki, Marin J. "Our Ally, Our Problem: Pakistan Is an Exceptionally Hard Case—Here's What to Do." *National Review* 54, no. 12 (2002): NA.

Weymouth, Lally. "Pakistan's Power Game; Former Leader Benazir Bhutto on the Tumult in Islamabad." *Newsweek* (2007): 35.

PHOTOS: Associated Press, Getty Images

VENEZUELA

"Deciphering Chavez's Psyche Is Not an Easy Task." *Miami Herald* (Miami, FL) (2007): NA.

"Narcotics Strategy: International Narcotics Control Strategy". Edited by Embassy of the United States, Caracas, Venezuela, 2003.

"Pulling the Plug; Freedom of the Press in Venezuela." *The Economist (US)* 383, no. 8531 (2007): 14US.

"The Rise of The 'Boligarchs'; Venezuela." *The Economist (US)* 384, no. 8541 (2007): 30US.

"Venezuela's Wrong Turn." *National Review* vol 46, no. n15 (1994): p18(2).

Corrales, Javier. "Hugo Boss: Ever Heard of a Regime That Gets Stronger the More Opposition It Faces? Welcome to Venezuela, Where the Charismatic President, Hugo Chavez, Is Practicing a New Style of Authoritarianism. Part Provocateur, Part CEO, and Part Electoral Wizard, Chavez Has Updated Tyranny for Today." *Foreign Policy* no. 152 (2006): 32(9).

Falcoff, Mark. "The Chavez Challenge: Venezuela's Leader Is a Regional Nuisance." *National Review* 57, no. 15 (2005): 37.

Gott, Richard. *Hugo Chávez and the Bolivarian Revolution*. London: New York: Verso, 2005.

Halvorssen, Thor. "Hurricane Hugo: Venezuela's Hugo Chavez Is a Threat to More Than Just His Own People." *The Weekly Standard* 10, no. 44 (2005): 25(3).

Johnson, Reuben F. "When Hugo Met Vladimir; Venezuela and Russia Are Up to No Good." *The Weekly Standard* 11, no. 44 (2006): NA.

Katayama, Lisa. "Sex Trafficking: Zero Tolerance." *MotherJones.com*. www.motherjones.com/news/dailymojo/2005/05/sex_trafficking.html.

Kozloff, Nikolas. *Hugo Chávez: Oil, Politics and the Challenge to the United States*. 1st ed. New York, N.Y.: Palgrave Macmillan, 2006.

Levin, Judith. "Hugo Chávez." *Modern World Leaders* (2006).

Marcano, Cristina, Alberto Barrera, and Kristina Cordero. *Hugo Chávez: Venezuelan President and Provocateur*. New York: Random House, 2007.

Morsbach, Greg. "Venezuela Aims for Biggest Military Reserve in Americas." *The Guardian*, March 4, 2006.

Rhem, Kathleen T. "Defense Ministers Express Concerns over Venezuela." *American Forces Press Service*. www.defenselink.mil/news/newsarticle.aspx?id=1415.

Schwartz, Stephen. "Troubling Roots: How Did Islamic Radicalism Grow in Guyana?" *The Weekly Standard* (2007): NA.

Sierra, Sandra. "Venezuela Eyeing Russian-Subs Deal." *Associated Press*, June 14, 2007.

Urbancic, Frank C. "Venezuela: Terrorism Hub of South America?" Paper presented at the House Committee on International Relations, Subcommittee on International Terrorism and Nonproliferation, Washington, DC (2006).

Wagner, Sarah. "U.S.-Venezuela Military Cooperation Indefinitely Suspended." *Venezuelanalysis.com*. www.venezuelanalysis.com/news/1085.

Zuckerman, Mortimer B. "The Devil and Mr. Chavez." *U.S. News & World Report* 141, no. 13 (2006): 64.

PHOTOS: Royal Canadian Mounted Police, Associated Press, Agência Brasil

SYRIA

"Assad's Unsurprising Victory: Syria Re-Elects Its President; To No One's Surprise, Bashar Assad, the Sole Candidate, Retains the Presidency." *Global Agenda* (2007): NA.

"A Damning Finger Points at Syria's Regime; The UN Report on Who Killed Lebanon's Former Leader; The Finger Points at Syria." *Global Agenda* (2005): NA.

"Rumours of War, and Peace; Israel and Syria." *The Economist (US)* 384, no. 8542 (2007): 37US.

Abrahms, Max. "When Rogues Defy Reason: Bashar's Syria." *Middle East Quarterly* 10, no. 4 (2003): NA.

Azarva, Jeffrey. "Getting Serious About Syria: It's Time to Stop Sending Mixed Messages to the Assad Regime." *The Weekly Standard* (2006): NA.

Babbin, Jed. "Regime Change, Again." *NationalReviewOnline.com*. www.nationalreview.com/babbin/babbin200311120817.asp.

Butcher, Tim. "Israelis Impose Blackout Over Syria Airstrike." *The Daily Telegraph*, September 21, 2007.

———. "US Confirms Israeli Air Strike on Syria." *The Daily Telegraph*, September 12, 2007.

Leverett, Flynt. "How to Get Syria out of the Terrorism Business." *The New York Times* (2003): A19.

Lieberman, Joe. "Al Qaeda's Travel Agent." *Wall Street Journal*, August 20, 2007.

Long, Rob. "Travels with Nancy." *National Review* 59, no. 7 (2007): 43.

Perthes, Volker. "The Syrian Solution." *Foreign Affairs* 85, no. 6 (2006): 33.

Salhani, Claude. "Syria at the Crossroads." *Middle East Policy* 10, no. 3 (2003): 136(8).

Schenker, David. "Assad State of Affairs: Syria's Dictatorship Survives to Fight Another Day." *The Weekly Standard* 11, no. 37 (2006): NA.

———. "Been There, Done That; Engaging Syria Isn't Going to Work." *The Weekly Standard* 11, no. 45 (2006): NA.

———. "Why Syrian Elections Matter . . . Even Though They Aren't Much of a Horserace." *The Weekly Standard* (2007): NA.

Schiff, Zeev. "Dealing with Syria." *Foreign Policy* (1984): 92(21).

Smith, Lee. "A History of Violence: Syria Reminds Lebanon of Their 'Special Relationship.'" *The Weekly Standard* (2007): NA.

Steinitz, Yuval. "The Growing Threat to Israel's Qualitative Military Edge." *Jerusalem Issue Brief* 3, no. 10 (2003).

Wurmser, Meyrav. "Up to No Good: Iran and Syria's Sinister Mideast Offensive Strikes Gaza and Lebanon." *The Weekly Standard* (2007): NA.

Zisser, Eyal. "Bashar Al-Assad's Gamble." *Middle East Quarterly* 13, no. 4 (2006): 61(6).

PHOTOS: U.S. Navy, Yuri Kozyrev/Columbia Journalism Review, *Time* Magazine, Veterans Memorial Museum, Al Jazeera

SUDAN

"Amnesty International Says China, Russia Supplying Arms Used in Darfur." *International Herald Tribune*, May 8, 2007.

"Darfur Conflict Spills into Chad." *The Christian Science Monitor* (2007): 6.

"How the UN Can Stop Genocide in Darfur." *Africa Action*. www.africaaction.org/newsroom/index. php?op=read&documentid=1603&type=15&issues=1024.

"Hundreds Killed in Attacks in Eastern Chad; U.N. Agency Says Sudanese Militia Destroyed Villages." *The Washington Post*, April 18, 2007.

"Possible AQ Presence in Darfur." *UN Confidential Report* (2007).

"Security Council Authorizes Establishment of 'Multidimensional Presence' in Chad, Central African Republic, Unanimously Adopting Resolution 1778 (2007)." *M2 Presswire* (2007): NA.

"Sudan: Arms Continuing to Fuel Serious Human Rights Violations in Darfur." *Amnesty International*. http://web.amnesty.org/library/Index/ENGAFR540192007?open&of=ENG-SDN.

"Terrorism in the Horn of Africa." *United States Institute of Peace: Special Report*. www.usip.org/pubs/specialreports/sr113.html.

Boot, Max. "Send in the Mercenaries; Darfur Needs Someone to Stop the Bloodshed, Not More Empty U.N. Promises." *The Weekly Standard* (2006): NA.

Cheadle, Don, and John Prendergast. *Not on Our Watch: The Mission to End Genocide in Darfur and Beyond.* 1st ed. New York, N.Y.: Hyperion, 2007.

Daalder, Ivo H. "Time to Intervene in Sudan." *Center for American Progress*. www.americanprogress.org/issues/2004/08/b137947.html.

Dallaire, R. "Looking at Darfur, Seeing Rwanda." *The New York Times,* October 4, 2004.

de Waal, A. "Tragedy in Darfur: On Understanding and Ending the Horror." *Boston Review,* October/November (2004).

Doyle, Mark. "Sudan's Interlocking Wars." *BBC Online.* http://news.bbc.co.uk/2/hi/africa/4759325.stm.

Englin, David L. "Plan of Action." *The New Republic Online.* http://ssl.tnr.com/p/docsub.mhtml?i=express&s=englin080604.

Evans, Gareth. "Darfur Needs Bolder International Intervention." *International Crisis Group.* www.crisisgroup.org/home/index.cfm?id=3468.

Farah, Douglas. "The Role of Sudan in Islamist Terrorism: A Case Study." *International Assessment and Strategy Center.* www.strategycenter.net/research/pubID.156/pub_detail.asp.

Flint, Julie, Alexander de Waal, and International African Institute. "Darfur: A Short History of a Long War." (2005): XIV, p. 152.

Gassis, Bishop Macram Max, and J. Stephen Morrison. "Sudan Impact: The Crisis in Sudan." *Hoover Institution.* www.hoover.org/publications/uk/3001746.html.

Henry L. Stimpson Center. "Future of Peace Operations Program." www.stimson.org/?SN=FP20040908717.

Hoge, Warren. "26 Nations Call for Sending U.N. Peacekeeping Force to Darfur. (Foreign Desk)." *The New York Times* (2007): A5(L).

International Crisis Group. "A New Sudan Action Plan." *Africa Briefing.* www.crisisgroup.org/home/index.cfm?l=1&id=3391.

Jacobson, Michael. "Navigating the Sudan Sanctions Regime." *Policy Watch/Peace Watch.* www.washingtoninstitute.org/templateC05.php?CID=2629.

Karl, Jonathan. "Dead End in Darfur? Robert Zoellick's Frustrating Mission to End the Genocide in Sudan." *The Weekly Standard* 11, no. 13 (2005): NA.

Kristof, Nicholas D. "Mr. Bush, Here's a Plan for Darfur." *The New York Times* (2007): A19(L).

Leonardi, Cherry. "'Liberation' or Capture: Youth in Between 'Hakuma' and 'Home' During Civil War and Its Aftermath in Southern Sudan. (Report)." *African Affairs* 106, no. 424 (2007): 391(22).

Marchal, Roland. "Creeping Conflict." *The World Today* 63, no. 4 (2007): 20(2).

Office of the Coordinator for Counterterrorism. "Country Reports on Terrorism 2006."

Patey, Luke Anthony. "State Rules: Oil Companies and Armed Conflict in Sudan." *Third World Quarterly* 28, no. 5 (2007): 997-1016.

Prendergast, John. "Genocide in Sudan?" *Policy Watch/Peace Watch.* www.washingtoninstitute.org/templateC05.php?CID=1763.

Prendergast, John, and Colin Thomas-Jensen. "Blowing the Horn." *Foreign Affairs* 86, no. 2 (2007): 59.

Reeves, Eric. "Current Proposals for Responding to Genocide in Darfur: A Compendium and Critique of Suggestions from the International Community." www.genocidewatch.org/sudancurrentproposalsforrespondingtogenocideindarfur23sept2004.htm.

———. "Genocide without End? The Destruction of Darfur." *Dissent* 54, no. 3 (2007): 8(6).

———. "Regime Change in Sudan." *The Washington Post*, August 23 2004.

Rice, Susan, and Eric Posner. "Will the International Community Act in Darfur?" *NPR.org.* www.npr.org/templates/story/story.php?storyId=6368478.

Rice, Susan E., Anthony Lake, and Donald M. Payne. "We Saved Europeans. Why Not Africans?" *The Washington Post*, October 2, 2006.

Rubin, Michael. "Engaged to Terror." *Jerusalem Post*, June 11, 2002.

———. "Sudan Hides Its Regime of Terror Behind a Mask of Diplomacy." *Daily Telegraph*, October 19, 2001.

PHOTOS: Espen Rasmussen/*Agence France-Presse,* Annie Sundberg/Ricki Stern, *Logos, Mother Jones*

NORTH KOREA

"Can They Do It? A Brief History of Resistance to the North Korean Regime." *One Free Korea.* http://freekorea.us/2007/03/06/can-they-do-it-a-brief-history-of-resistance-to-the-north-korean-regime.

"Nakasone Proposes Japan Consider Nuclear Weapons." *The Japan Times*, September 6, 2006.

"North Korea: Limited Options." *National Review* 55, no. 1 (2003): NA.

"Tempting Mr. Kim: Dealing with North Korea, Continued. (Six-Party Talks Over North Korea Finally Resume)." *The Economist (US)* 384, no. 8538 (2007): 41US.

Timeline: North Korea Nuclear Stand-Off. 2007. http://news.bbc.co.uk/2/hi/asia-pacific/2604437.stm.

Timeline: North Korea's Nuclear Weapons Development. 2004. www.cnn.com/2003/WORLD/asiapcf/east/08/20/nkorea.timeline.nuclear/.

Berkowitz, Bruce. "Is Assassination an Option?" *The Hoover Digest* Vol. 1 (2002).

Blumenthal, D. "Facing a Nuclear North Korea and the Future of U.S.-R.O.K. Relations." ICAS Fall Symposium (2005): Washington, DC.

———. "Kim Jong Il, Rocket Man; Time to Defuse Him." *The Weekly Standard* 11, no. 41 (2006): NA.

Bolton, John R. "Pyongyang's Perfidy." *The Wall Street Journal Eastern Edition,* May 18, 2007: A17(1).

Derbyshire, John. "Kim Jong Il: A Modest Proposal." *NationalReviewOnline.com.* www.nationalreview.com/derbyshire/derbyshire040403.asp.

Eberstadt, Nicholas. "The Most Dangerous Country." *The National Interest* (1999): 45.

———. "North Korea's WMD Program: Purposes and Implications." *American Enterpirse Institute.* www.aei.org/publications/pubID.21992,filter.all/pub_detail.asp.

———. *The North Korean Economy: Between Crisis and Catastrophe.* New Brunswick, NJ: Transaction Publishers, 2007.

Eberstadt, N., and J.P. Ferguson. "The North Korean Nightmare." *Weekly Standard* 9, no. 47 (2004): 22–30.

Frum, David. "Mutually Assured Disruption." *The New York Times* (2006): A25(L).

Gittings, Danny. "China Props Up an Evil Regime." *Asian Wall Street Journal*, January 16, 2003.

Goldfarb, Michael. "The Next Test; North Korea Now Claims It is Building a Hydrogen Bomb." *The Weekly Standard* (2006): NA.

Haggard, Stephan, and Marcus Nol. "Skidding into a Deal." *Newsweek International* 150, no. 12 (2007): NA.

Henry L. Stimpson Center. "Reducing Nuclear Dangers in South Asia." www.stimson.org/southasia/?sn=sa2001112043.

Kaplan, David E. "The Far East Sopranos" *U.S. News & World Report* (2003): 34.

Kristof, Nicholas D. "Escape from North Korea." *The New York Times* (2007): A19(L).

Kurlantzick, Joshua. "Look Away—A Do-Nothing Korea Policy." *The New Republic* (2003): 14.

Lee, Sung-Yoon. "Aggressive North, Submissive South; What Bush Can Do for the People of Korea." *The Weekly Standard* 11, no. 45 (2006): NA.

Mazzetti, Mark, and David E. Sanger. "Raid on Syria Fuels Debate on Weapons." *The New York Times* (2007): A1(L).

Plesch, Dan. "Without the UN Safety Net, Even Japan May Go Nuclear." *The Guardian*, April 28 2003.

Pritchard, Charles L. *Failed Diplomacy: The Tragic Story of How North Korea Got the Bomb.* Washington, D.C.: Brookings Institution Press, 2007.

Robbins, Carla Anne. "Wrestling Nuclear Genies Back into the Bottle, or at Least a Can." *The New York Times* (2007): A24(L).

Rubin, Michael. "Dangerous Cycle: North Korea, Iran, and Repetitive Diplomatic Failure." *American Enterpirse Institute.* www.aei.org/publications/pubID.24626,filter.all/pub_detail.asp.

Schell, Jonathan. "Talks Without End." *The Nation* 281, no. 11 (2005): 10(1).

Stelzer, Irwin M. "Guns and Butter: How the Bush Administration's Fiscal Policy Has Narrowed Its Options in the Realm of Foreign Policy." *The Weekly Standard* (2006): NA.

Steorts, Jason Lee. "Axis Uber Alles? Bush is Not Dealing Adequately with Iran and North Korea." *National Review* 59, no. 8 (2007): 26.

Telenko, Trent. "North Korea's Tony Sopranos." *Winds of Change.net*. www.windsofchange.net/
archives/002967.php.

Triplett, William C. *Rogue State: How a Nuclear North Korea Threatens America*. Washington, D.C.: Regnery
Pub., 2004.

Waldron, Arthur. "A Korean Solution?" *Commentary* 119, no. 6 (2005): 62(4).

PHOTOS: Artemii Lebedev, Associated Press, Martyn Williams, GlobalSecurity.org/Public Eye

Editor

STEPHEN ELLIOTT

Staff Writers

JASON ROBERTS, ERIC MARTIN,
ANDREW F. ALTSCHUL, PETER REDNOUR,
GREG LARSON, AND JESSE NATHAN

Research Fellows

JENNIFER KING

ALLY-JANE GROSSAN

JORDAN BASS

CHRIS YING

ALYSSA VARNER

MATT WERNER

CLAIRE POWELL

SHARAREH LOTFI

NICHOLAS BUTTRICK

GWENDOLYN ROBERTS

ADAM KREFMAN

ANNIE WYMAN

ELIZABETH BAIRD

ANDREW HEVIA

BRYCE GOODMAN

CHRIS LINDGREN

CHRISTOPHER BENZ

GRAHAM WEATHERLY